"Whatta-Gal"

"Whatta-Gal"

The Babe Didrikson Story

William Oscar Johnson and
Nancy P. Williamson

A Sports Illustrated Book
Little, Brown and Company   Boston – Toronto

JB
zah

FIRST EDITION

T 05/77

Babe Didrickson's letters to Ruth "Tiny" Scurlock are reprinted by permission
of the Mary and John Gray Library Collection of Lamar University, Beaumont,
Texas.

Library of Congress Cataloging in Publication Data

Johnson, William   1931-
    Whatta-gal!

    "A Sports illustrated book."
    1. Zaharias, Babe Didrikson, 1911-1956.
2. Athletes–United States–Biography. I. Williamson,
Nancy P., joint author.   II.   Title.
GV697.Z26J63   796'.092'4[B]   76-56812
ISBN 0-316-46943-2

*Sports Illustrated Books
are published by
Little, Brown and Company
in association with
Sports Illustrated Magazine*

Published simultaneously in Canada
by Little, Brown & Company (Canada) Limited

PRINTED IN THE UNITED STATES OF AMERICA

"Whatta-Gal"

Chapter
1

Babe Didrikson Zaharias
(1911–1956)

She was kissed by greatness at a dangerously early age, but she was blessed with a rare true grit that worked to make her whole life a singular event, ultimately even heroic. Her name is no longer a household word; she has been dead now for twenty years. But on the September morning in 1956 when she died of a particularly grotesque and painful form of cancer, President Eisenhower opened a press conference at the White House by saying: "Ladies and gentlemen, I should like to take one minute to pay a tribute to Mrs. Zaharias, Babe Didrikson. She was a woman who in her athletic career certainly won the admiration of every person in the United States, all sports people over the world. I think every one of us feels sad that finally she had to lose this last one of all her battles." There was a genuine grief in his voice; Ike had been a good friend of Babe.

The New York *Times* published an editorial that said: "Babe Didrikson Zaharias has finally lost the big one. This one was the hardest to lose, but she knew that 'You can't win them all,' and that there is one antagonist against which even the stoutest heart is not quite defense enough."

Intimations of mortality came to millions on the day Babe Zaharias "lost the big one." Many people could not remember a time when her long jaw, her Roman nose, her wide, delighted smile had not appeared regularly in their newspapers. Her fame reached back to the summer of 1932, a cataclysmic season for the United States. The veterans' bonus riots in Washington had become so violent that President Herbert Hoover had effectively locked himself in the White House. The gates were chained and padlocked, and policemen roamed the grounds. The country was falling into the pits of the Depression of 1932, yet Hoover continued to dine each evening in black tie, surrounded by footmen and butlers. He did this on the premise that the nation would lose respect for the presidency and for itself if he did not maintain this pose. But the hungry and the poor were so desperate that many people predicted a new American revolution before the year was out. More than fifteen million people were out of work. Newspapers constantly carried stories about men who committed suicide because they could find no way to support their families.

Against this bleak backdrop, Babe Didrikson's star rose, and she experienced personal triumph so intense that only a few human beings – prime ministers, presidents, generals, astronauts – ever come near it. Her name was known from coast to coast, around the world. Newspapermen nicknamed her "Whatta Gal." Many declared her to be the greatest woman athlete in history; some called her the greatest athlete – man or woman – ever to live on earth. On July 16, 1932, Babe had entered the national amateur athletic track meet for women in Evanston, Illinois, and *by herself,* she won the national woman's *team* championship. Two weeks later, in Los Angeles, she won two gold medals and a silver at the Olympic Games. Headlines bloomed in colossal bouquets across the country:

Babe Breaks Records
Easier Than Dishes

Babe Gets Great Praise On
Coast: Is Called Greatest
Woman Athlete of World

On the morning of August 11, 1932, she flew back from the Olympics to her home state of Texas. The Postal Department had given special dispensation for the mail plane of American Airways to dip low over Dallas and circle the downtown district. When the plane and its escort ships were sighted, sirens on office buildings and whistles on factories sent up a cacophony to signal her return. Ten thousand people were waiting at Love Field. Her hometown newspaper, the Beaumont *Journal*, reported the occasion with a five-column headline on Page One:

Babe, Heralded Like Lindbergh or Big Dirigible Akron,
Planes into Texas in Sailor Pants Carrying Three Javelins

The lead paragraph said: "With her progress ticked off on press wires as if she were Lindbergh, the Prince of Wales or the dirigible Akron, Babe Didrikson, the 19-year-old Beaumont girl who went, saw and conquered the world of athletics at the Olympic Games in Los Angeles arrived over Texas soil by airplane Thursday morning. . . ."

The morning paper in Beaumont, the *Enterprise,* ran a larger front-page headline:

World Famous Babe Is Given
Tumultuous Dallas Welcome
Amid Ticker Tape Showers
Tells of having picture
taken with Clark Gable

A dozen bands came to the Dallas Airport to march in Babe's parade. When she stepped out of the mail plane, she was wearing a sailor cap on her bobbed hair. She wore a shirt with the U.S. Olympic emblem on the chest and a pair of flaring baggy beach pants. She moved with the lithe unconscious arrogance of a panther. The crowd roared at the sight of her. The Dallas Police Department band struck up "Hail to the Chief." Dozens of local dignitaries were there to say hello. One of them, wearing a limp white suit and perspiring beneath his straw hat in the rising morning heat, introduced her to the crowd as "the Jim Thorpe of modern women athletes." The crowd shouted and clapped. People reached to shake her hands, to touch her. Only Charles Lindbergh had ever been given such a massive reception in Dallas. Yet Babe accepted hers with an aplomb that was almost nonchalance. She looked as if she were convinced that if Jim Thorpe were being introduced somewhere that day he would be called "the Babe Didrikson of male athletes."

When a reporter asked her if she had anything to say, Babe replied, "I want to say hello, that's all." The crowd cheered. She said. "I brought back eight first-place medals of gold and one second-place medal of silver and a bronze medal for fourth place. I made eight world's records in the last month and I am terribly happy." Someone asked about her future and she replied, "I am definitely going to enter the national golf tournament for women in Massachusetts next month and, what's more, I believe I'll win it. I can outdrive most women golfers now and I've only played ten rounds of golf in my life." Someone asked her why in tarnation she was traveling with *three* javelins and she grinned and said, "Well, I got even with somebody. I took one discus out there and somebody hooked it, so I swung onto these three javelins. I come out ahead, don't you-all think?" The crowd laughed. People were excited. Not many of them had ever been so near an airplane; even fewer had seen a legend up so close.

Statistics form the spine of the legend of Babe Didrikson Zaharias. This is true of nearly all athletes: the results of sporting events are finite, almost never abstract. In most other human pursuits, in art, music, literature and so forth, greatness is a matter of intangibles. But in sports there are winners and losers; the results are unmistakable; the statistics are immutable. In the case of Babe, the statistics that define her greatness are so impressive they seem almost too good to be true.

Between 1930 and 1932 she held American, Olympic or world records in five different track and field events. During the A.A.U. national meet of 1932, she entered as the sole member of the Golden Cyclones, a team sponsored by the Employers Casualty Company of Dallas; Babe scored thirty points in the meet. The next best team, the Illinois Women's Athletic Club, had twenty-two members who scored a total of twenty-two points.

In the Olympics at Los Angeles, she won gold medals and set world records in the 80-meter hurdles and the javelin – breaking the javelin record by an astounding eleven feet. She tied for first place in the high jump, setting another world record; officials ruled, however, that she had dived illegally during her last successful jump and she was awarded the silver medal instead of the gold.

She was an All-American basketball player in 1930, 1931 and 1932, and led her team, the Golden Cyclones, to the national championship in 1931. She often scored thirty or more points a game in an era when twenty points for an entire team was a respectable total. She was an excellent softball player who pitched and batted over .400 in a Dallas city league. Later, she pitched for the itinerant bearded baseball team of the House of David. She appeared in a few major league exhibition games, pitching for the St. Louis Cardinals, the Philadelphia Athletics and the Cleveland Indians.

As a golfer, professional and amateur, she won eighty-two golf tournaments. In the mid-1940s she won a record seventeen consecutive tournaments, capping that string in 1947 by becoming the first American to win the British Ladies' Amateur Championship. In 1954, only fifteen months after undergoing radical surgery for cancer of the rectum, she won the United States Women's Open at Peabody Country Club in Salem, Massachusetts, by a shattering *twelve* strokes, a record never broken.

She was an excellent bowler with a 170 average. She could punt a football seventy-five yards. She won tennis tournaments in Beaumont and Dallas and a diving championship in Beaumont, and she could swim very close to world record times in short distances.

Six times – in 1932, 1945, 1946, 1947, 1950 and 1954 – she was voted Woman Athlete of the Year by the Associated Press. In 1950, the Associated Press picked her as Woman Athlete of the Half Century. (The male was the brilliant Indian athlete Jim Thorpe, who by then had become a fat and alcoholic man who would die penniless three years later, in a trailer in Homita, California.)

Friends and disciples of Babe Didrikson Zaharias have been eager to gild her legend. They swear that she excelled at an assortment of sports so enormous and so diverse that it is suspect. A man who acted as Babe's chief journalistic admirer, from the early years of her career at Beaumont High School, was William "Tiny" Scurlock, a three-hundred-pound Texan who was sports editor of the Beaumont *Journal*. Tiny Scurlock adored Babe, much as if she were a singularly lovely and successful daughter. He collected clippings about her, he saved her letters. When Tiny Scurlock died he bequeathed a large filing cabinet full of memorabilia about her to the library at Lamar University in Beaumont. Tiny included in that collection his own rough and loving biographical notes about her. They are typed on smudged sheets of wire service copy paper. In part, Tiny recorded small personal things about her: "She is an excellent dancer, her favorite color is blue. She likes chicken legs and fish in a big way, but she doesn't like mutton at all. Her main weakness in school was talking in class, but she was always protecting underdogs." Mostly Tiny Scurlock compiled a growing, glowing report of games and sports at which she excelled: "She was a crack shot with her rifle when a kid and could knock a sparrow from the peak of a barn or a telephone line with ease. She was croquet, checkers and dominoes champion of her neighborhood, a fine archer, an excellent horsewoman, captain of her own rollerskate hockey team, a good water polo player, ice skater, surf boater, canoeist, skeetshooter, billiards and pool player, boxer, wrestler and polo player." Tiny reported that he had interviewed a Beaumont man named Will Fort, a shipyard worker who had once operated a bowling alley, and that Will Fort told him: "The Babe came in to bowl for the first time and I showed the Babe how to approach the line and that was all she needed. In her very first game that girl bowled one hundred and ninety-three." Tiny reported that Babe shot a 91 the first time she held a golf club in her hands and that once, playing for her high school basketball team, she scored 99 points (forty-seven field goals, five free throws) in one game.

All of these things were set down with loving care, but many of these "facts" were inflated by the affection big Tiny Scurlock felt for Babe. Others, too, have written Babe Didrikson somewhat larger than she was in life. The sports writer Frank G. Menke once dug through a burial ground of yellowed clippings and tattered box scores to come up with the shimmering statistic that as an amateur athlete Babe entered 634 competitions and was victorious in 632 of them. This, too, was purest loving balderdash. Yet it is the measure of her legend that many people do not doubt the truth of such fictions.

If the spine of her legend is built of statistics, the soul is made of memories. They are warm and inexact, the lovely opposite of statistics. There is immense vitality in the memories about Babe – so much vitality that they come near to bringing her back from the dead. Her joie de vivre, her vigor still seem actually to exist among the people she touched. They still see Babe as a lean and talkative young woman, full of fun and pranks, tough sometimes, a hustler, a huckster, yet loving and generous, gentle, joking. Although their reminiscences of Babe are charged with youth and promise, they have changed, they have aged, and the contrast between the exuberant scenes they evoke in memory and the weary realities of today can be startling, even sad.

From shirttail childhood through the moment of her death, no one was closer to Babe Zaharias than her older sister Lillie, Mrs. O. B. Grimes. Lillie was sixty-six in the spring of 1975, two years older than Babe would have been. For the past forty-one years, Lillie lived in the same tiny white bungalow on Roberts Street in Beaumont. A widow since 1969, Lillie had become a plump and sweet old lady with wispy gray hair. She wore rimless spectacles that sometimes flashed in the sunlight when she laughed, or grew misty when she wept. Lillie Grimes seemed left behind by the world, a refugee from a more tender time when everyone she loved was still alive. "You know what Babe liked more 'n almost anything?" asked Lillie. "Ridin' on the Ferris wheel. Oh, my, we would ride 'em by the hour, Babe and me. That was after she come into money, we couldn't afford no Ferris wheel rides before. But, oh, how that girl would *work* for things she wanted. When I was livin' with her in Dallas, I wasn't but twenty, twenty-one, she was just learnin' golf. Babe, she'd hit and hit the balls until she had to put tape over her hands. Oh, she was *so* tore up, but Babe, she wouldn't *stop*. I'd be out there with her and I'd be so *hungry*. It'd be gettin' dark, and I'd *beg* Babe to go in, but she'd say, 'No, I got to hit just a few more, Lillie.' And she'd hit 'em so *far* and she'd ask me where they went and I'd say 'Babe, *I* don't know where they're goin'. It's dark. I ain't no *Indian,* Babe.' "

Lillie wandered in her conversation sometimes and was forgetful, but her ambling memories of Babe seemed more important to her than her own life now. She said, "We all lived over on Doucette Avenue and Papa built the house. It's all colored there now. Sometimes I'm real anxious here, too, 'cuz colored's movin' in over back of me on that other street, I can't think of its name. I remember once my mama sent Babe to the store to get some meat. Instead of takin' it right home, Babe went to the old Magnolia schoolyard to play some game – baseball, I suppose. She set that ol' meat down and when she finished the game it was gone. You know, some big ol' dog must've took it. Babe she had to go home without it. My mama was real mad, oh, my, she was real mad. We wasn't real rich in them days, I tell you, and my mama she *spanked* Babe. She used a broom. But then my mama couldn't stand it and she hugged Babe up. She loved us all so much, my mama did. And Babe. Oh, that Babe. She could do anything. She'd make the prettiest maps in Geography. Some of us copied 'em from her. We had such good times, Babe and me . . ."

Babe's husband, George Zaharias, was a robust good-looking giant when she married him in 1938, a professional wrestler who became a celebrated villain. George's stock act was to break into cowardly tears when the hero of the match began to win; he came to be known as The Weeping Greek from Cripple Creek. George was frequently at Babe's side during golf tournaments, an unforgettable figure who ultimately ballooned to almost four hundred pounds. When interviewed in 1975, George Zaharias was ill, emaciated and feeble, confined to bed most of every day. He was seventy years old. He had been crippled by a massive stroke. His eyesight was almost gone. A pacemaker had been installed in his chest. When he spoke, his voice was husky and weak, although it seemed to take on strength when he talked of Babe. They had met at the Los Angeles Open in 1938. "It was a beautiful sunny day," recalled George, "and we teed off early in the morning. She was wearing a light brown sweater and a pleated skirt with pockets. I had wrestled in Beaumont and I'd heard she was the greatest thing that ever lived. When I read the pairings, I said, 'I don't want to play with no girl,' but I was kidding. I liked her the first minute I saw her. I put my arms around her in a wrestling hold for the photographers. She said, 'This is great.' I said, 'You're mine, you know that.' She said, 'That's right.' I'd been playing golf for only about a year and I was shooting in the eighties. I was nervous, but mainly because I thought I might hit someone with the ball. Babe teed off first and she blasted it. I hit one so far left that the ball landed on another fairway, but we both made birdies on that first hole. She said, 'Well, I see you're a player, too.'

"We chitchatted – you know, athlete to athlete. And we really got along. I finished with an eighty and she shot an eighty-one. We had some beers. She drank German beer, an expensive one, and I told her, 'Hey, you're livin' high on the hog.' She said it cost only a thin dime more. She liked champagne. She liked it all sugared up. She'd stir it around and get it to *sing*. I took her to dinner at a Hollywood restaurant, the Black Swan, where they cooked steak on top of a coal stove. It wasn't honky-tonk. There were no shows or anything, just an out-of-the-way restaurant I'd found. For two-fifty you got a big steak, potatoes, salad. Oh, yeah, everything was OK with everyone right from the start. I was wrestling every night. I was not dating anyone else. Nothing was held back. We were engaged in November. I bought this diamond, you know, a two-carat ring, and I said to her, 'This will make some girl happy.' Babe laughed and said, 'That would make *me* happy.' We were living together in an apartment in St. Louis, but we never seemed to find the time to get married. I kept telling her it would only take five minutes. Finally, I said, 'Babe, we can't go on like this. You're too *famous* to be living together.' So we got married just before Christmas in 1938. We had a party afterwards and we had champagne. Babe made the champagne *sing* that night."

Ruth Garrison Francis Scurlock was eighty-one in the spring of 1975. Many years ago, in the late 1920s, she was a young English teacher at Beaumont High School and Babe Didrikson was one of her students. Ruth Scurlock knew Babe well at school and got to know her even better in later years because Ruth married Tiny Scurlock, the sports editor of the Beaumont *Journal.* In 1975, Ruth Scurlock hobbled about on two canes in her cool and spacious Beaumont home. She was a cultured, articulate woman, an expert on Texas history, and her sitting room had a full wall of history books and texts, mostly on this subject.

She spoke about Babe one night in May 1975 as the ceiling fans turned lazily to ward off the heat. "Babe's skin was tanned and very soft; it was lovely skin, not like a lizard's, the way so many of these Texas women golfers get to be. She had that lovely skin and she also had smooth, rippling muscles. There was nothing knobby or knotted about her calves. She had a typical Norse grace. She was a classic, slender Norsewoman, not masculine at all. I remember Babe came to dinner here at our home one night. She loved cars and at that time she had a magnificent long tan Auburn. She parked it in our driveway. It was a splendid, shining thing, with exhaust pipes on the outside of the hood. The children from the neighborhood heard our famous Babe was here and they gathered outside, chattering and rubbing the fenders of the car as if it were some kind of idol. They kept coming to the front door clamoring for Babe to 'come out and play.' I told them, no, they had to wait until we had finished dinner. After we finished eating, Babe did go out and she was with those children for two hours, teaching them to hold golf clubs or swing tennis racquets or bats or whatever they brought over with them. She was with them until long after sunset. Oh, how she loved children. Then the next day, she left for a tournament somewhere in Arkansas. She loved to drive very fast, and in Louisiana, just across the Texas state line, she hit an old man coming out of his driveway in a wagon. She killed him, I think. There was some litigation over it, but Babe had good lawyers and she got out of it all right."

Bertha Bowen and her husband R. L., of Fort Worth, were close friends – really second parents – of Babe from the mid-1930s on. They were very wealthy, both well into their late seventies in 1975, and they happily recalled how they used to take Babe and George fishing at their cabin in Colorado. Bertha said, "Everything was competition with Babe. She loved trout fishing – she probably liked it even more than golf – but it was competition. One time she said she'd go one way down the creek and we were to go the other and whoever got the most fish would win – ten dollars or a free dinner or whatever. Well, George and I and R. L. had real good luck and we were sure that this time we beat her. But, no, no, wouldn't you know, here comes Babe strolling up the path with a willow stick over her shoulder and the darndest string of trout you've ever seen. She'd beaten us, all right, but you know – those were a kind of fish that didn't grow in that river. I don't know where she got 'em. She never told us, but it's my guess she bought 'em off some guy who was stocking the river." R. L. chuckled and said, "Babe was a real scaredy-cat though in the woods. I remember one time she was standing in the woods, hollering like crazy for George. She was terrified because this beaver had surfaced in this pond and whacked the surface with its tail. She was so scared, she had tried to run away, fallen down and broken her fishing rod. She really had a very sensitive nature. She loved fish, but she wouldn't even eat a bird or a quail, let alone hunt them. George was queasy about animals, too. Once we were fishing in Colorado and we found George, deathly pale, sitting on top of a fence gate. He was shuddering and he said, "A goddam *bear* came after me!' It turned out it was only a cub, but he was so shaken that we had to stop the car so he could be sick."

In the relatively short span of her life, Babe came to know men and women from every level of society, every kind of background – millionaires, movie stars, boxing champions, army generals, Damon Runyonesque characters who hung around the fringe of sports. She knew Amelia Earhart intimately and admired her courage but raved even more about the fact that she had "the most beautiful hands in the world." She refused to be in a movie *(Pat and Mike)* with Spencer Tracy and Katharine Hepburn until the script was changed to let her beat Hepburn at golf. She became fond of Tracy and liked Hepburn, although she found her a bit overbearing and told friends, "Kate's double-parked with herself." She often visited Ike at the White House and her standard breezy greeting to him was, "Hey, Mr. President, how's Mamie's golf?" She once beat Babe Ruth out of two hundred dollars in a distance-driving contest and embarrassed a bashful young slugger named Ted Williams by consistently outdriving him in front of a group of reporters. She bowled with Harold Lloyd, the celebrated silent-movie comedian, played tennis with movie stars John Garfield and Paul Lukas, golfed with the likes of General Omar Bradley, Joe Louis, Bing Crosby and Bob Hope. She was also a friend of hundreds of anonymous, unglamorous people who remember her with great love. One such was Sid Marks, a short, heavyset fellow with hair white as an Easter bunny, pink freckled skin, a gnarled nose that was broken fifty or sixty years ago when he boxed under the name of Seaman Sid the Barroom Brawler. He was seventy-five in 1975, and he worked as a chief security guard in a twenty-four-hour poker casino in the weary Los Angeles suburb of Gardena. Sid Marks was an associate of George Zaharias when George was a wrestling promoter at the old Olympic Arena. He adored Babe. "Ah, Babe, she was always tootling away on her harmonica," said Sid Marks. "She and George had a house on Van Ness in L.A. after they were married, you know. She said to me one day, 'Sidney' – she called me Sidney – 'do me a favor? I have lots of clippings stored here in boxes. Sidney, if I give them to you, will you paste them up for me?' I told Babe, of course. I would do anything for Babe. I got some scrapbooks, they're big as a whole cardtable top, you know. Babe brought this box – and a really deep box, it was – I was glad I had brought lots of paste. I started working on that scrapbook. I emptied the box of clippings, but I had to start another book. Babe said, 'Sidney, I have a few more clippings,' and she brought in another very large box. I said, 'Babe, I gotta get another scrapbook.' I brought two more back with me. And more paste. I'm bending over Babe's table, pasting and filling the pages. We get down to one mountain of clips in a box. I almost fill a third book. I'm maybe eighty-five pages in, and then she brings me *another* big box of clippings. She said, 'Here, Sidney, George found these, too.' So I have to go back down to the arena and get another scrapbook. I was bent over that table to fill *four* scrapbooks full of clippings – the *paste* I used! When I finished, I couldn't straighten up my back. I had to go to the Pico Baths and get a massage and a steam before I was all right again from Babe's scrapbooks. She made me dinner then, Norwegian meatballs, that's what she cooked best. And she tootled on her harmonica."

Babe's main claim to being the greatest woman athlete lies in the diversity of the sports she performed, but her fame at the end of her life – and most of the one million dollars she made – came from golf. Naturally, her closest friends in sports came to be golfers. Patty Berg was as famous as Babe thirty years ago. Patty was then stout and freckled, a childlike woman who had become a professional golfer in 1940. Patty Berg was fifty-seven in 1975. Her curly red hair was speckled with white and she wore spectacles. She was the grand dame of golf, certainly, but she looked more like a sweet old grandma, and her recollections of Babe rambled pleasantly: "One night we were staying together on the tour and Babe told me she was not sleeping well. She went on and on about how she couldn't ever get a night's sleep. We checked into a motel near Miami and we were both tired. We left everything in the car and went to bed. Babe wakes me in the morning with this awful shout, 'My God! My purse is gone.' I leap up. My wallet is gone, too. Babe is running around saying all her money is gone and they've taken her gold watch. I said, 'Babe, if you're such a poor sleeper, how did they get in here?' She had nothing to say. We go down to breakfast and all of a sudden Babe whispers to me that she knows who did it. She's staring at the maitre d' and she's *convinced* he's the one because he's wearing shoes with rubber soles. I talked her out of that. Next, we go to the car, and, sure enough, they cleaned that out, too, except for one shoe. I wish you could have seen the expression on her face, standing there holding up one shoe. I phoned my insurance company and she kept whispering in my other ear, 'Ask 'em if your insurance covers me, too.' "

Peggy Kirk Bell, fifty-three years old in 1975, was a tall, tailored woman who, with her husband Warren owned and operated the plush Pine Needles golf course in North Carolina. Peggy Bell met Babe Didrikson Zaharias on the golf tour in 1945 and they were warm friends until Babe died. Peggy recalled: "When I had my first child, Babe told me to name the baby after her. I said, 'But, Babe, you hate the name Mildred.' Babe did not have Mildred in mind, she wanted my baby called 'Babe Bell' because it would look so great in print. She was always worried about what was going to look good in print. Babe told me, 'I'll teach her how to play golf. Don't you mess her up, she's going to be the greatest golfer in the world.' I had wanted a boy, but Babe was delighted it was a girl. 'All boys are good athletes,' she said. 'But there aren't many girls who are. Girls can become great athletes easily.' When the baby was born, Babe was up in Washington having lunch with Ike and said she just had to leave because her good friend was having a baby. She rushed down here the night the baby was born. She tore into the hospital. 'Where's that baby?' she yelled. In a few minutes, she had the place turned upside down. She kept saying, 'Get the photographer in here. Where is the doctor? Where is the press conference?' There I was, half alive, and Babe was setting up pictures. She thought everything she did was news.

"The first time I met Babe, I was so excited because here was this great track star, the great Didrikson. We met at the Western Open in Indianapolis in the locker room. Babe said, 'Come on, kid, I'll play you some gin rummy.' I didn't know how to play. She said, 'That's okay, I'll show you how to play,' and the next thing I know she is madly adding up something on a piece of paper and she tells me the game is over and that I owe her twelve dollars. Then she said, 'Listen, I'll give you a chance to win it back.' I said no thanks. For years, I always teased Babe about how she hustled a green kid out of twelve dollars. She always said, 'Oh, I never did that.' But she did. She was always on, always entertaining, always laughing. We'd sit down to eat and she would balance a spoon on her hand, whack it and jump it into a glass. She'd hit a cigarette and catch it in her mouth. When she was dying in Galveston, she was still going to entertain you. I went to visit her and she said, 'See that Coke bottle over there?' And then she promptly flipped a cigarette into it. She was always doing the impossible. If she missed, no one remembered. When she made it work it became legend."

No one loved Babe more at the end of her life than Betty Dodd, a tall thin woman from San Antonio. She was only nineteen when they first met at a golf tournament in 1951; Babe was forty. They became instant friends. They had golf and music in common (Betty was a splendid guitar player and singer; Babe's harmonica playing was absolutely professional). Betty and Babe began a friendship that lasted through the lingering horrible days that preceded Babe's death. Betty Dodd was forty-four in 1975, a friendly, open woman who obviously still missed Babe deeply. She said, "Babe was a barrel of fun to be around. She had a little two-dollar harmonica, it was the only one she knew how to play – but she could make her own sharps and flats on it, cheap as it was. We made a record for Mercury – played 'Detour,' it was Babe's favorite song after 'Begin the Beguine.' She loved jelly beans. One time some guy sent her fifty pounds of them and they were in the trunk of the car for months. There was hardly room for her golf clubs. We had such wonderful times. I would have walked underground to China for Babe in those days. She was the most famous person in the world and I was her protégé.

"The last time I saw her was eleven days before she died. She weighed only eighty pounds and we talked about the victims in the concentration camps and how they too were down to eighty pounds and they came back. Babe knew that she must look like a concentration camp inmate. Young interns would come in to see her, they couldn't believe she was still alive. They kept saying she should have been dead five months ago. Her muscle structure was unbelievable. Her will to live was so great she just wasted away to nothing; it was a very slow death. She had so much muscle, such vitality and was in such good shape, it took time to wear her down. When she died, I reacted very strangely. It was like a burden being lifted. When you care so much for a person and see her in such horrible pain, dying so slowly, it is a relief when she is finally dead."

That she died so young was tragic but Babe's life was spectacularly well lived, filled with an intensity of experience that few people have. Wherever she went, Babe made the champagne sing and the children laugh. She was an enthusiast, an entertainer, and she lived in an aura of immortality from the time she was a very young woman. Yet her era was unsympathetic to women and, as a female athlete, she was seen by many as a freak. She was insulted, ignored, laughed at. This made her tough, even bullying at times. Sportswriters referred to her as a "muscle moll" and even her good friend Paul Gallico wrote about her as a member of a breed of "women who made possible deliciously frank and biological discussions in the newspapers as to whether this or that woman athlete should be addressed as Miss, Mrs., Mr. or It."

She survived such denigration with stoicism or humor. Yet she did react to it – eventually. In her youth, she was outspokenly disdainful toward "sissy women" frills. Later she became more overtly feminine. She let her hair grow long. Though she dressed with good taste usually, her only errors in the selection of clothes occurred when she wore things too frilly. For years after most women on the golf tour wore Bermuda shorts, Babe stuck with skirts. As she grew older, her physique took on more womanly proportions. As the heroine of the

Olympic Games, she was slat-thin and flat-chested; she weighed one hundred and twenty-eight pounds and was five feet, seven inches tall, a whippetlike athlete. Later she filled out, weighing around one hundred and sixty when she was at the top of her golf game. She became downright bosomy (38-C). This was an occurrence that she viewed as a mixed blessing: once when she missed a spare during a bowling game, she came back gesturing at her breasts and shouting, "God*damn* these things! They sure do get in the way." She was very strong, but when she was older she went out of her way to conceal it. Occasionally she forgot herself. Once at a Miami country club in the early 1950s, a short heavyset man with a thick neck and a powerful simian build sat next to her at the bar and began tapping her on the shoulder, constantly interrupting her conversation, generally annoying her. Babe said to him, "Listen, if you don't stop I'm going to do something about it." He snarled at her, "Yeah, you and that four-hundred-pound husband of yours." Babe said, "I don't need him." She flipped the fellow flat on his back and pinned him to the floor. It was strictly a reflex action and she was embarrassed once it was done, ashamed.

She was the greatest female athlete of her time – almost certainly of all time – and she could never deny the physique that made her that. If there was ambivalence about her proper role or appearance as a woman it grew from society's strict and narrow interpretation of what the proper woman *should* be. Proper is one thing, natural another, and everything that was natural about Babe led her to sports, traditionally a man's world, and that made her a rebel, albeit an unconscious one. She was not a feminist, not a militant, not a strategist launching campaigns of sexual liberation. She was an athlete and her body was her most valuable possession. Her instincts led her to use it to its utmost and that made her a legend while she was still alive. It was

never easy though and Babe Zaharias's battle to excel was –
symbolically, at least – the same one all women have been fighting:
for the right to be equal, the right to be natural. As her old friend and
schoolteacher Ruth Scurlock said, "Babe was a very brave girl or she
could never have become the person she was."

Chapter 2

Perhaps it would seem excessive to speak of "bravery" in someone who happened to be enormously talented at athletics and then proceeded to excel at it. Yet for a woman to do so required a great deal of courage, determination – and bravery. For centuries, the accepted way for women to exert power has been through indirection. The image of feminine influence on the world has long been associated with coyness, wile, deception, flirtation – the Woman-Behind-the-Man syndrome. Women who break this mold have been scorned; they are considered unseemly, pushy. Sport is the antithesis of the traditional model for women, for it is aggressive, forward, definitely pushy. Sports insist on a directness of purpose: no coquette ever stole second base, no shy maid ever flirted through a 100-yard dash. Sports demand the behavior that tradition reserved for men. Women in sports threaten the status quo; they explode the roles of the sexes that have been accepted through the aeons.

Let us pause briefly in the story of the greatest woman athlete to place her in the history of women. For, of course, Babe was a product – as well as a victim – of the times in which she lived.

In the seventeenth century the generally accepted role of the female was characterized by a clergyman named Thomas Fuller, who said: "A woman is to be from her house three times; when she is christened, married and buried." A natural rebellion against such unnatural restraint began to build. In 1848, the country's first convention for women's rights was held in Seneca Falls, N.Y., and the nation was scandalized by the group's major resolution: "Be it resolved that men and women are created equal." From this the American campaign for emancipation began, but it was tiring, slow, discouraging. Every instinct, every tradition, every institution was against it. For example, in 1869, a woman named Myra Bradwell passed the Illinois bar examination but was not allowed to practice because of her sex. Miss Bradwell appealed to the United States Supreme Court and the Court said no: "The natural and proper timidity and delicacy which belongs to the female sex evidently unfits it for many of the occupations of civil life." The issue of giving women the right to vote was bitter, as divisive nationally as the later racial conflicts of the 1960s. Women themselves denounced the movement. Actress May Irwin, the "Toast of Broadway" in the 1900s, said: "I am sick to death of this shrieking for women's rights. It is doing more harm than good among women. I have more rights now than I can properly attend to." And a magazine called *The Woman Patriot* wrote: "The suffragists are bringing us to the culmination of a decadence which has been steadily indicated by race suicide, divorce, break-up of the home, and federalism, all of which conditions are found chiefly in primitive society." Nevertheless, on August 26, 1920, the Nineteenth Amendment was at last passed and twenty-nine million women were enfranchised to vote. It was only the barest official beginning of equality, a grand legal step but one that did little to change the prevailing opinion that women's role was one of docile obedience, of domestic servitude.

Sports, adventure, and vigorous physical exercise were absolutely man's domain. There had been over the years a few female daredevils who went against the currents. In the 1850s Amelia Bloomer appeared in public wearing an outfit consisting of a skirt and ankle-length underpants, which soon came to be called "bloomers." It was a scandal, but it was a tiny essential first step toward releasing woman from the bondage of clothing. The feminist Elizabeth Cady Stanton reported on the joys of physical exercise after wearing Ms. Bloomer's apparel: "What incredible freedom I enjoyed! Like a captive set free from his ball and chain, I was always ready for a brisk walk through the sleet and snow and rain, to climb a mountain, to jump over a fence, work in the garden, and, in fact, for any necessary locomotion."

Freedom of locomotion was an incomparable aid to women who enjoyed sports, but it took decades after the bloomer breakthrough before women were allowed to be effectively unfettered for exercise. When Mary Outerbridge, of Staten Island, New York, introduced the game of tennis to the United States at the Staten Island Cricket and Baseball Club in 1874, the typical costume included an upholstered corset, starched petticoat, starched skirt, a long-sleeved blouse with high collar, a four-in-hand necktie, a belt with a silver buckle and sneakers with large silken bows. As late as 1919 Suzanne Lenglen, the French tennis player, appeared on a tennis court wearing a short-sleeved, one-piece pleated skirt over shorts – with *no* petticoat – and she was criticized for being indecent. That year Ethelda Bleibtrey, a competitive swimmer who would win three gold medals in the 1920 Olympic Games, stripped off her stockings before going for a swim on a New York City beach and was cited for "nude swimming."

A few women performed feats of derring-do that caught the public eye and even some public praise. The famed Nellie Bly went around the world in 1890, in seventy-two days, six hours, eleven minutes and fourteen seconds and her accomplishment was ballyhooed and much admired as the first "Tour of the World by an Unattended Woman."

In 1901 grade-school teacher Annie Edson Taylor amazed the world by becoming the first person to survive a trip over Niagara Falls in a barrel. In 1911, Annie Smith Peck made the first ascent of Mt. Coropuna in Peru and announced she did it because she wanted to stand at a height where "no man had previously stood." Despite such courageous aberrations by individuals, organized sport at the turn of the century was almost entirely male-dominated, a profane and muscular world of spikes and spittoons where women were not welcome as participants and not particularly encouraged as spectators. Like the grounds of battle, the fields of sport had not been created by God for the weaker sex. This, of course, had been tradition since time unrecorded. During the Olympics of ancient Greece, women were executed if they appeared as spectators. In Rome they were allowed to look but never to participate. There was one period, in the dimmest days of civilized life on earth, when women may have been the reigning stars of sport. On the island of Crete, thirty-five hundred years ago, there was a kind of rodeo sport known as bull-jumping. As depicted in murals from that time, the event was performed by an athlete who stood in front of a charging bull until a split second before contact, grabbed the tossing horns, executed a whirling handspring over the bull's back and landed safely on the ground just beyond the animal. The athletes in these paintings were women.

As the prosperous halcyon first days of the twentieth century dawned there was the beginning of a new popularity in women's sports. Many women still cultivated pale faces, laced themselves into corsets ten inches too small (the "Wasp Waist" was de rigueur) and thought croquet too strenuous, but at the same time America produced its first all-around woman athlete – Eleanora Sears. She was a woman whose versatility and feats of daring were not surpassed until Babe herself came along. Born in 1881, Eleo, the daughter of a Boston shipping magnate and great-great-granddaughter of Thomas Jefferson, excelled in horseback riding, tennis, squash, swimming, sailing, marathon walking and even polo. In 1905 she was fined for driving without a license; in 1910 she was one of the first women to go up in an airplane; and two years later she drove a four-in-hand coach down Manhattan's Fifth Avenue on a cold January morning to win a twenty-five-dollar bet. She introduced and frequently wore riding britches, a practice considered so sinful that sermons were preached against her and in 1912 a Burlingame, California, Mother's Club passed a resolution saying, "We hereby put ourselves on record as strongly opposed to the unsightly mannish attire worn by Miss Sears and request that she restrain herself in the future to normal feminine attire." Delighted, Eleo promptly adopted shocking outfits for swimming, sailing, figure skating and tennis. In her lifetime she won more than two hundred and forty trophies, including four national tennis titles from 1911 to 1917. She was a crack shot with a rifle and pistol and as a teenager she played baseball, hockey and football, where she starred as a fullback. She also boxed. In her later years she thought nothing of walking from Boston to Providence, a fifty-mile trip. She was a frequent dancing partner of the Prince of Wales but her true love was sport. "I began exercising the first time I fell out of my crib and I don't plan to stop until I'm in my coffin," she said. In 1968 Eleonora Sears died at the age of eighty-seven. Her athletic zest and competitive spirit had paved the way for women's entrance into sports at the turn of the century.

Women's basketball, which was started at Smith College in 1891, rapidly became the most popular sport of the period and by the 1920s a majority of American public schools had teams. Other sports such as speed skating and bowling also attracted thousands. In 1920 America sent its first women's team – swimmers – to the Olympics in Antwerp. In 1922 the United States Field Hockey Association was formed and for the first time a women's track team was sent to an international meet in Paris, where they finished second to Great Britain.

Thus in the 1920s, when Babe Didrikson was growing to adolescence in Beaumont, the American climate was actually more promising for young women in sport than it had been for centuries. But there were strange influences in the land during the decade of the 1920s. It was a weird and rudderless time, a kind of historical hurricane eye between the ghastly battles of World War I and the onrushing catastrophe of the Depression. Warren Gamaliel Harding, a vapid, handsome man given to "bloviating" (his own term for windbag pronouncements), became President in 1921 and though he died after just twenty-nine months in office, his lax administration had already presented the country with the Teapot Dome scandal. Next came Calvin Coolidge, who served until 1929 in a musty atmosphere of disinterest (during his White House stay, Coolidge made it a point never to miss a two- to four-hour nap after lunch). Against the bankruptcy of such pallid leadership excesses bloomed: the sheiks and shebas of Flaming Youth launched their reckless burst of hedonism, while supermoralists and raving evangelists damned their antics and deplored their morals. The Ku Klux Klan had an enthusiastic rebirth and the country was fraught with fads and zany sensations. Everything seemed exaggerated, supercharged, overwrought.

Given this background of excesses perhaps it is easier to see how a relatively mild and basically enlightened campaign to revise the national view of women's sports could career so far out of control that it effectively wrecked female athletics in America for nearly fifty years. There was, in the early 1920s, a perceptible trend toward elitism in all sports – women's, too. In order to produce winning teams many schools were favoring only the best players while relegating ordinary competitors to the sidelines or to the bleachers. This was anathema to many people, and a powerful group of women began a formal campaign against it in 1923.

It was led by Mrs. Herbert Hoover, wife of the Secretary of Commerce in the Harding and Coolidge administrations. A brilliant woman who spoke five languages, Lou Hoover organized a group called the Women's Division of the National Amateur Athletic Federation. The Women's Division was founded to propagate an idea well conceived and certainly well intentioned. Mrs. Hoover described the plan in a founding pamphlet:

A team for everyone and everyone on a team! This is the aim of the new plan for athletics among girls. Athletics need no defense. It has long been established as part of our school system. Only those who make the winning teams, however, have heretofore had the full enjoyment of athletics. . . . Many know how to watch a few play to the grandstand, but do not themselves know how to participate even when there is no grandstand to inspire or intimidate as the case may be.

The basic argument against elitism in athletics was and is a viable stand, responsible, necessary. Elitism in men's sports in the United States has been the cause of all manner of hypocrisy, corruption and warped values. It has been responsible for recruitment scandals in colleges, sub rosa payments to "amateur" athletes. It has caused the elevation of the "winning is everything" philosophy (a bankrupt idea if there ever was one) to a level of religion. It has spoiled children's fun through overorganization of recreational outlets such as Little League baseball, football and hockey. Elitism in sport has effectively removed fun from games for millions of Americans. It has come to be an American shibboleth that the raison d'être of sport is to excel rather than to enjoy. Obviously this tends to make *play* become *work,* and obviously that is a serious distortion of values.

Thus the crusade of the Women's Division was well intended, but over the long run it caused untold damage. Michigan State University physiologist William Heusner recently said:

By 1940 it had been carried far beyond any rational expectation. Some of the professional leaders in women's physical education (people who should have known better) actually seemed to deny girls their biological heritage of vigorous physical activity. Marriage and re-production were practically the only "acceptable" social-physiological outlets for young women. The financial depression of the 1930's with its resulting scarcity of industrial jobs reinforced this unfortunate trend. The old expression "a horse sweats, a man perspires but a woman merely glows" was typical of the attitude. Intramural sports developed and flourished but there still was no avenue open for the highly skilled girl to realize her potential within the education framework. As a result, countless young women turned to club and industrial teams which operated without the benefit of educational leadership and standards.

What happened was that the Women's Division mixed up its enlightened argument against elitism with some mossy tenets of sexism. Its campaign began turning on the fact that the weaker sex should be demure and take its exercise out of the public eye, that competition on an interscholastic level was all right for men but not for women, that women were biologically unfit for hard athletic competition. At its second convention in 1925, Mrs. Hoover's Division passed by a 72–2 vote a resolution calling for the outlawing of all forms of "extra-mural competition" for women: they opposed gate receipts for women's games, all travel for women to sports events, all publicity about women in sports. The Division gathered powerful support. The National Association of Secondary School Principals issued a declaration backing the Division:

Inherent evils in interscholastic competition among girls demand its suppression. These evils are so patent that they do not require much discussion. The extremely strenuous physical and mental exertion and strain are a menace to girls in the high school period. Furthermore, sooner or later, the spectacle of interscholastic contests among girls gives rise to undesirable and even morbid social influences among both boys and girls and in the community life as well.

In 1926, the Women's Division held its annual meeting at the Hotel Astor in New York and a spirit of celebration prevailed. They opened the convention with an evening highlighted by group lessons from Henry Ford's personal dance instructor, accompanied by Ford's personal orchestra. The next day, the Division listened to a lengthy progress report from Executive Secretary Lillian Schoedler. Overall, she was optimistic: "I would say there is not a *very* great deal of *destructive* work, comparatively, being done throughout the country in girls' athletics. Track and field athletics, and swimming offer possibilities for exploitation and overdoing which are not being altogether missed." However, the sport of basketball stood as a scandal, a monumental threat to women's virtue. Miss Schoedler read a long list of basketball horrors: girls going off on four- or five-day trips; girls fainting during games; girls being "bought up" by men scouts to play for certain teams. She declared there were far too many "championship-thirsty" people and she attacked all basketball tournaments for women because of "the nervous strain and excitement, the tendency which such games breed to disregard physical safeguards, to play during menstrual periods and to play beyond the effort a girl ought to make, [and because] the type of audience often involved mixed groups whose attitude and comments are anything but constructive. They are problems, these keenly competitive basketball games. . . ."

Miss Schoedler attacked industrial basketball leagues, saying that firms often hired girls who had no qualifications except their athletic prowess. She attacked chambers of commerce and other civic groups for using girls' basketball teams to improve their city image: "This type of exploitation is little, if any, better or different from the bathing beauty type of exploitation – and there is little question about the stand of sane leaders regarding that!" And she attacked – of all things – Sunday Schools and churches for their sponsorship of women's basketball:

It is certainly to be regretted that such institutions are forming so black a chapter in the story of girl's athletics, and that institutions which ought to stand strongly for high ideals and constructive standards are permitting so much that is undesirable or even harmful to take place under their patronage, for the sake of increasing their constituency or popular prestige.

After this convention, Mrs. Hoover resigned as president of the Women's Division. Her departure did not curtail the crusade; indeed, it became more zealous if anything. The attack on women's basketball went on relentlessly, but the group now also went after track and field, plus the most sacrosanct of all sporting events, the Olympic Games.

The Division felt that the Olympics were the pinnacle of athletic elitism, which is true enough. But instead of pursuing their campaign on this sound ground, the Division again veered off into blatant sexism. Ethel Perrin, associate director of the American Child Health Association, expressed the Division's sentiments by declaring: "Girls are not suited for the same athletic programs as boys. The biological difference between them cannot be ignored unless we are willing to sacrifice our school girls on the altar of an Olympic spectacle. Under prolonged and intense strain a girl goes to pieces nervously."

In 1929, the Division went on record as being opposed to the participation of girls and women in the 1932 Olympics. They recommended that instead of sending a women's team to the Games in Los Angeles, the United States should send a group of women there "for the opportunity of putting on in Los Angeles during the Games (not as part of the Olympic program) a festival which might include singing, dancing, music, mass sports and games, luncheons, conferences, banquets, demonstrations, exhibitions, etc."

A year later the Division drafted a petition to the president of the International Olympic Committee, M. Le Compte de Baillet-Latour. It said, in part:

Whereas, Pierre de Coubertin, founder of the modern Olympic Games said to the Athletes taking part at Amsterdam in the IXth Olympics [1928] Games, "As to the admission of women to the Games, I remain strongly against it," and, Whereas it is the understanding of the Women's Division, National Amateur Athletic Federation, that it is within the power of this International Olympic Congress to vote the participation of women in track and field events in the Xth Olympiad at Los Angeles, California, USA in 1932, Therefore the Women's Division petitions this International Olympic Congress to vote to omit track and field events for women from the 1932 program.

Nothing happened to change the Olympics as a result of the petition except that the 800-meter race for women was dropped. Obviously the powers of the Division were not as effective beyond the borders of the United States. Yet, at home – in scarcely seven years – they had effectively squelched high-level competition for girls in nearly all American high schools and colleges. Because of the Division and the thousands of unenlightened physical education professionals who went along with it for so many years, competitive women's sports in the United States were so effectively crippled that they are only now, in the decade of the 1970s, beginning to approach the level of popularity that existed when the Division was formed. Had this powerful group never intervened, it is possible that women's sports might have boomed and ballooned and gotten rich on a par with men's. There would have been recruiting scandals for women, a female Vince Lombardi or George Allen to lash women on to the Ultimate Victory, player strikes and multimillion-dollar lawsuits in the women's professional leagues. It might have been a mixed blessing, but it would have been equality. And though there has been only one woman in this century with Babe Didrikson Zaharias's inspiring record, there might have been more if the disparagement of women's athletics had not been so widespread and so intense. Indeed, Babe herself might have been just another Mildred if she had not managed to match up her splendid physique with a remarkably fierce spirit and an uncommon portion of good luck. Neither history nor her own origins made her life easy.

Chapter
3

She was born Mildred Ella Didriksen in Port Arthur, Texas, on June 26, 1911. The year of her birth was something Babe sweetly obscured, and the resulting confusion is on display at her gravesite in Beaumont. On her tombstone, carved in marble, the years of her life appear as 1911–1956. On an official Texas historical marker, stamped in steel, at the entrance to her burial plot, it says the year of her birth was 1914. That is the date she used in her autobiography, *This Life I've Led*. On her application for the Tenth Olympiad in 1932, Babe wrote in a penciled girlish scrawl that she was born in 1913. In the early 1950s, she claimed the year to be 1915, and once, when she applied for a visa, she declared it was 1919. There is no birth certificate on file at the Jefferson County courthouse. However, sister Lillie had a baptismal certificate that listed the date as 1911. Lillie declared, "I don't know what Babe said, but I went to a lot of trouble to get it right on the gravestone. I figured that's goin' to be there till the hereafter and I wasn't goin' to have it wrong."

Thus, the fabled Whatta Gal was not nineteen as everyone thought, but twenty-one when she captured her medals in the 1932 Olympics. That she performed her feats as a legal adult instead of a bouncing teenager perhaps slightly diminishes the size of her legend, but it does not matter. Nor does it matter that she always spelled her last name with an "s-o-n" while her parents used "s-e-n." Babe explained the discrepancy by saying, "I wanted everyone to know I was a Norwegian, not a Swede." But the fact is that *sen* is more common in Norwegian usage than Swedish.

Her father, Ole Nickoléne Didriksen, emigrated from Norway in 1905. He was a small, wiry seaman with a large straight nose, square shoulders and large ears, a ship's carpenter who had sailed around Cape Horn nineteen times before he settled on dry land for good. Ole chose the dank, hot town of Port Arthur on the Gulf of Mexico as his new home; he had been there once on an oil tanker. Years later, Ole Didriksen told a surprised reporter that he had selected Port Arthur "because I liked the climate." It was a fetid, semitropical sort of land, the terrain covered with the ugly paraphernalia of the oil drilling industry, which was then newly booming in East Texas. The celebrated Lucas gusher, first of the massive oil strikes in that part of the country, had blown like a volcano in 1901 a few miles out of Port Arthur on a section of ground known as the Spindletop. It had flooded the land for hundreds of acres around in a black lake of oil. By the time Ole Didriksen arrived, the Spindletop was producing millions of barrels of oil each year.

He lived alone in Port Arthur for three years. This was the decade of the twentieth century that saw an unprecedented flood of immigrants arrive in America – 8,795,386 between 1901 and 1910. Many of them had fallen on hard times and Ole wanted to prove he could subsist before he brought his wife and three children to America from Oslo. He became a furniture refinisher, an odd-job carpenter at the port. He was a skilled craftsman; his father had been a cabinetmaker in Oslo, and Ole had learned to do everything with wood, from making intricate tiny ships inside bottles to building beautifully fitted cabinets. He once rebuilt the chassis and frame of a rusty Model T Ford with mahogany. He built a house in Port Arthur for his family, a sturdy place that resembled the interior of a ship, with built-in cabinets and concealed cupboards. The house stood until 1962, when it was demolished by the owner, a Port Arthur architect named Guy Edwards. He said the house had become an "eyesore," but he added: "The material and work was comparable to the Babe – everything was first class. Even if you could afford some of the lumber Ole used, you couldn't get it. There were two-by-fours twenty-two feet long and straight as an arrow, marked with the code letter 'B' which designated the best material available."

One of the first ornaments Ole Didriksen put on his new house in Port Arthur was a flagpole. It poked out from beneath the eaves and he hoisted an American flag up there every day. Ole said, "I'm a Norwegian but nobody's a prouder American than I am." Unlike other immigrants who came to America to seek – and make – a fortune, Ole Didriksen was a man without driving ambitions or dreams. He never made much money and was content to putter about with other people's furniture or work on varied construction projects. He was satisfied with a relatively minimal, unadorned style of life; his favorite aphorism to his children was: "Get plenty of exercise and keep your bowels clear."

In 1908, after he had worked three years to prove he could make a living in Texas, Ole Didriksen summoned his wife, the former Hannah Marie Olson who was the daughter of a shoemaker in the medieval city of Bergen. She came to Port Arthur from Oslo with her three small children – Ole, Dora and Esther. Hannah Didriksen was a pale, fragile woman who wept easily or laughed with giddy abandon as the mood struck her. On the muggy day she shepherded her children to their new life in Port Arthur, the mood that struck was bleak indeed. The port waters were filled with shabby oil tankers and the shore was a clutter of raw-lumber buildings. Everywhere there were oil rigs, the clanking sound of machinery, the smell of oil. The population of Port Arthur seemed to consist entirely of oil-stained roughnecks. Coming fresh from the clean, ordered land of Norway, Hannah Didriksen was overwhelmed by these sights and she began to weep. Lillie Grimes said, "My mama, she told me that she couldn't believe what she seen – nothin' but oil, oil, oil [this was pronounced "awl, awl, awl" by Lillie] and she just couldn't stand it. My mama, she cried and cried and cried to think she had left beautiful, beautiful ol' Norway for this."

The shock was profound indeed, and, in a way, Hannah Didriksen never recovered completely. She remained uncomfortable, an alien in the United States. Outside her home, she was shy, bewildered. She never learned to speak English fluently. Lillie recalled her through tears and chuckles: "Oh, my mama, she couldn't understand lots of what went on around her. She liked her kitchen best of all. She was such a little short thing and she got her English and Norwegian mixed up, but she was always laughin' and, oh, she loved us so much."

She went about baking bread, scouring pots, having babies – four more of them. The house Ole Didriksen built in Port Arthur was on Seventh Street, a street as banal as its name. Most of the tiny cement-block-mounted bungalows on Seventh Street were owned by the Gulf Oil Company. The "awl, awl, awl" that Hannah had grieved over on her arrival was already the economic backbone of dozens of East Texas towns. However, oil workers did not prosper greatly, or live very well. Oil money was rarely used to beautify their environment or to enrich their lives. It either went to develop new wells or into the pockets of men who were already millionaires many times over. The Didriksens lived in Port Arthur for seven years after Hannah arrived in America.

In 1909 she bore twins, Lillie and Louis. In 1911 there was Mildred Ella, and in 1915 came Bubba, the last. By then the family had roots on Seventh Street and the children who were old enough went to school less than a block from home.

On August 16, 1915, the birth date of little Bubba, all this was violently uprooted. The baby was born in a bedroom of the house hours before a savage hurricane struck the Gulf Coast. It was one of the worst storms in history. Monstrous tides rampaged through Port Arthur; winds up to 120 miles an hour tore up trees and toppled church steeples; 275 people died and the damage was more than $55 million. Terrified, the Didriksen family waited as their sturdy little house held firm against the winds, then watched in horror as it slowly filled with surging floodwater. Lillie was six years old and she recalls: "We was so scared. The baby was born and we left that house behind right away. Everything was gone in the flood. Ducks, chickens, trees, beds, money, dishes, everything. We didn't save nothin'. We just got out of town."

Ole Didriksen took his frightened family seventeen miles up the road to Beaumont. They found refuge there with other victims of the storm and waited until the weather cleared.

There must have been a vein of poetic irony in the carpenter and his wife, for they christened their newborn son Arthur Storm Didriksen.

Beaumont became their home. It was no Eden either. The Didriksens moved to the South End, a seedy part of town. They rented houses for a time until, at last, Ole bought another home on Doucette Avenue. It was a busy, noisy street. A trolley line ran down the center and the trolley barn was two blocks away from the Didriksen home. At one end of Doucette were railroad tracks where rumbling freight trains, made up mostly of tanker cars, rolled constantly north. At the other end of the street was Beaumont's largest industrial complex, the

Magnolia Refinery. It sprawled there like a Martian junkyard, steam and odors pouring out of its pipes and chimneys. God only knows what dark vapors people breathed around the Magnolia Refinery in the days Babe was growing up. Air pollution was unknown and, thus, unfeared, but the atmosphere was probably full of poisons; as recently as the early 1960s, pollution in Beaumont was so bad that women's nylon stockings disintegrated on their legs as they walked on the city streets.

The refinery employed almost everyone on Doucette Avenue and was referred to with respectful familiarity as "The Magnolia." It was the economic life-force for all of Beaumont, omnipotent and omnipresent. All big business in America in the early twentieth century was considered to have almost religious powers; as Calvin Coolidge once said, "The man who builds a factory builds a temple, and the man who works there worships there." The Magnolia was no exception; it was Beaumont's Vatican. The Magnolia owned the only radio station in town. It had its own basketball team which played itinerant clubs like the Celtics or the House of David; it built the school – Magnolia School – on Doucette Avenue. It controlled the town's politics. It owned most of the housing for many blocks around the refinery.

Of course, oil money and oil influence were relatively new to Beaumont in those days when Babe Didrikson was growing up on Doucette Avenue. The town had subsisted largely on lumber and cattle through the nineteenth century. It was originally called Tevis Bluff when it was founded in 1823 and later came to be known as Beaumont, no one is quite sure why. It was always a hostile sort of territory; early horseback preachers traveling through called it the Alligator Circuit. The Neches River abounded with water moccasins, alligators, bootleggers and renegade families who lived on squalid houseboats deep in the swamps. In 1908, the year Ole Didriksen brought his family to Texas, the channel of the Neches River was deepened to allow oceangoing vessels to reach Beaumont; much of the work was done by sweating convicts wearing balls and chains. The discovery of oil on the Spindletop in 1901 had brought the port to life.

Despite its uncomfortable climate and its tough industrial look, Beaumont once was a town of certain social substance. Ruth Scurlock lived there since the turn of the century and she recalled: "It was in many ways a rather elegant place. There was the Beaumont Yacht Club where Harry K. Thaw and John D. Rockefeller used to dock sometimes in Rockefeller's yacht, the *Wild Duck*. In fact, Rockefeller came to Beaumont on his honeymoon. In the nineteenth century, there were flat-bottom side-wheelers in the river. Sam Houston came here once and bathed in the mineral waters of Sour Lake near town. There was an old Negro there who used to mix water and mud for facial packs and at one time people thought Beaumont might become the Saratoga of the South. There was lots of entertainment – the Alamo Café where ladies of light repute went upstairs with the customers. Fuller's Restaurant had fine seafood that they caught fresh themselves each day with their own fishing fleet. The Hotel Beaumont had the Rose Room and the Black Cat Coffee Shop and served dinner in its roof garden. On a clear night you could see all the way to Port Arthur; the oil rigs were lighted up like stars along the ground for miles.

"I am afraid now Beaumont has become a very banal town. It is a transient town with people from the oil companies living here for two years, then moving on. It was, once upon a time, what I would call a cultured, gracious town with good food, bridge games and a literary club. The Kyle Opera House had three balconies and the road companies used to go straight on to California without another stop once they had played Beaumont. Sir Harry Lauder played Beaumont. We saw *Birth of a Nation* here, *Tea for Two, The Red Mill* and *Rio Rita.* These things do not happen in Beaumont any longer."

Beaumont did produce a few celebrities besides Babe. Some are more impressive than others. Television star Fay Emerson was born there as was S. Perry Brown, national commander of the American Legion in 1948, the four Perricones, the first American quadruplets to survive infancy, and Frank Robinson, major league baseball's first black manager. Perhaps the best-known figure besides Babe was a lanky fellow whose father was director of the high school band. In 1932 he was sixteen and he approached an itinerant bandleader named Lawrence Welk to ask if he could try out as a trumpet player. Welk listened to the young man play, then shook his head and told Harry James, "No, you play too loud for my band, son."

When Babe Didrikson was growing up, her life on Doucette Avenue reflected little of the elegance and the culture that Ruth Scurlock recalled. The street was full of rednecks and roughnecks, hard-knuckled families living in washboard poverty. The Didriksens had a constant struggle to subsist, and Hannah sometimes worked as a practical nurse and sometimes took in washing. A couple of times Babe's father had to go back to sea for brief voyages to support the family. The older children all had jobs and before Babe was in her teens she had taken a job for thirty cents an hour at a fig-packing plant. Later she worked at a gunnysack factory, sewing up the sacks at a penny apiece; she made sixty-seven cents an hour – a very good wage then – and gave most of it to her mother to buy groceries.

The children Babe grew up with were hardy, shirttail urchins and there were dozens of them in the neighborhood. They played devilish games with the trolley cars on Doucette: they soaped the tracks so the trolleys slipped to a stop; they scampered up to yank the overhead wire off its track so the car moaned to a halt, forcing the motorman to climb to the roof and hook things up again; they sneaked aboard for free rides all over town. They swam in the treacherous Neches and somehow survived its snarling swift current and its vast population of reptiles. They played baseball with coverless balls wrapped in black friction tape and with fielders' mitts they got as free premiums with Octagon soap wrappers. Sometimes if they had a nickel they went to the movies – "the flickers" – and watched *The Adventures of Kathlyn White* or *The Iron Claw* or *The Perils of Pauline.* Sometimes, during World War I, they went to band concerts in a downtown park and listened to khaki-clad soldiers from nearby camps sing songs like "My Buddy" and "The Rose of No Man's Land." The Magnolia sponsored these patriotic concerts.

To some the South End of Beaumont may have seemed a hard place to live. But not to the Didriksens. Babe wrote in her biography: "It was just a wonderful family life we had there." And Lillie Grimes recalled those times as being nothing but idyllic days of endless sunshine and barefoot frolic.

As she reminisced, Lillie nodded her gray head, chuckled and wiped her tears. She had a great bedraggled scrapbook spread open before her and, as she spoke, Lillie paged through it, pausing to gaze at certain items, taking others in her hands. She held snapshots of Babe as a child, squinting into the sun toward the camera, and she said: "Babe liked roller skatin' the best. And she was the best at *ever'thing* we did. Oh, we was all *over* the streets, always gone from the house. We knew when it was supper time, all right, but we never paid no attention to nothin' else. Mama, she was always callin' and *callin'* to get us home. Babe was worst, she'd never come home unless it was dark or she was *real* hungry. She got the most spankin's 'cuz she was the most full of devilment. Oh, and she'd *pinch* me all the time 'cuz she'd get *mad* about havin' to wash the dishes. We always wanted to wipe, not wash 'em, like all kids, you know. We used to fight like cats and dogs. My papa, he built a mirror over the sink where we washed dishes so we'd have to look in there and see how sour and mad we looked when we was fightin'. We had this huge old porch on the house, just fulla windows, and that's where we had to wash dishes. That ol' porch, it went around two sides of the house with *sixteen* windows in it. Just *full* of sunshine all the time. My papa, he slept on the porch there 'cuz he *snored* so. My mama had a glass window put in between her room and Papa's place on the porch to keep away the awful noise he made snorin.' "

Lillie turned a scrapbook page and gazed at a photograph of Babe. She was in her mid-twenties, striding down a tree-lined street somewhere, and Lillie said, "Oh, my, say this here pitcher was taken by the aviator lady . . . you know who I mean?" Amelia Earhart? "Yes! Amelia Earhart took this pitcher up in Connecticut one time." Lillie turned a page and picked up a snapshot lying there. It was a color print of a wax mannequin of Babe in a Dallas museum: the figure was erect, corpselike, paralyzed in a golfing backswing. The hair was a garish inaccurate yellow. Holding this grotesque snapshot, Lillie prattled on lovingly about life long ago on Doucette.

"My papa, he put up a trapeze and all sorts of stuff in the big tree back of th' house and we pretended we was in the circus, hangin' by our feet, tryin' to hang by our teeth even. Across the street a lady lived, we called her Aunt Minnie. She was really in the circus, she really *did* hang by her teeth, Aunt Minnie did. One time, it was nineteen twenty-three or twenty-five I guess, and Aunt Minnie was goin' to go to California with her niece, our neighbor, and she talked my mama into lettin' Babe and me go along for a while. She thought

Babe might grow up to be a real good trapeze artist. We went in a big ol' open car on little tiny roads in the mountains; we was so scared. Babe learned to hang by her toes and turn flips in the air and walk the tightrope without no umbrella in California. We got to ride on a big elephant, he was the biggest in the world. I loved bein' on that big ol' thing, but for some reason Babe was scared. That's the only time I ever seen her afraid of somethin' that I wasn't. We went to school there for a while. We didn't learn a thing and when we got back to Beaumont, they put us back a grade."

Lillie turned the scrapbook pages. Yellow newspaper clippings, brown photographs rolled past. Babe in a mink coat and white gown; Babe in shorts and black anklets, hanging from a pipe; Babe in a football uniform – leather helmet, cleats. Lillie said, "That was make-believe. She played football when she was little, but she never got into no real tackle football games. We never played dolls that I can remember. All the neighbors had hedges, you know, and Babe she liked to practice the hurdles up and down the street. She went to ever' house and got 'em to all cut down their hedges to the right size. I could run faster 'n Babe sometimes, but I could never do them hurdles like she could. She got her nickname, you know, from playin' baseball. She hit so many home runs, that girl did, that someone said she was just like Babe Ruth and so that's how she got that name. Marbles, she was real good at. She won all the marbles in the neighborhood, that girl did. Oh, she was somethin', that Babe, she had the prettiest handwritin'. One time we hopped on a freight train, oh, we used to do it all th' time, but this one time I'll never forget. It started goin' faster 'n faster 'n *faster*. Babe hollered to me we had to git off, but I was so scared. She jumped off and then I couldn't make myself get off and Babe, she had to get back up on the car and push me off. Then she fell off, too. Oh, we was so scared, but we just got skinned up, we never got hurt no worse than that. One time me and Babe, we sneaked in the hospital and we took a look at a new baby there. Just to see what it looked like, you know. Oh, I don't know what they would've done if they caught us."

Lillie paused to look at a pearly gray photo of her beloved mama and papa in Norway, at a picture of a 1933 Dodge Babe once gave her father, at a newsprint picture of Babe and Yogi Berra, at a telegram of sympathy from Jimmy and Tommy Dorsey when Babe died. Lillie sighed. "There was always music, so much music in the house. My papa, he played violin pretty good. Esther and Dora played piano. My mama, she sang. And Babe, oh, Babe was just *somethin'* on the mouth organ. She could play that harmonica like nothin' you ever did hear. It gives me chills to remember how good Babe was and how we all sounded, singin' and playin' music in that ol' house my papa built. People used to turn out their lights in the other houses and come out and sit on their porches to hear us play and sing to 'em before they went to bed."

The house on Doucette still stood in the spring of 1975, sturdy and tight as the day Ole Didriksen finished it sixty years ago. However, it had not been painted in many years. The neighborhood had a listless look, too. Weeds grew long in sidewalk cracks, lawns were unmowed, some of them were littered with trash. The old Magnolia Refinery (now owned by Mobil Oil) still sprawled at the end of the street like some ageless natural entity – a mountain range or a forest. The trolley tracks were gone, but the railroad tracks at the other end of the street were not. In the vernacular of some people in Beaumont, Doucette Avenue was in the area called "Nigger Town."

One May afternoon Lillie Grimes and her son Jody, who was twenty-eight, an articulate and intelligent young man with a degree in psychology and a job with the oil company as a "mud engineer," decided to visit the place. Lillie strode up on the porch and knocked at the door. A black woman answered. Lillie explained that she was Babe Didrikson's sister and "we all lived here so many years ago and we had such wonderful times in this ol' house and we'd like to take a peek in again, to show my son where his famous Aunt Babe lived." A bit reluctantly, the woman opened the door. She said she was Mrs. Mildred Gibbs. She was slim, neat, well-spoken. She said she and her husband and their children had lived there five years. She kept apologizing for the unkempt look of the place, the boxes on the porch, the dishes in the sink, the clothing strewn about the parlor; Mrs. Gibbs explained that she had been ill. Lillie had not seen the house in twenty years.

She seemed to fall almost into a dream as she moved about, touching the woodwork done by her father, peering out a window into the backyard where she and Babe had swung from trapezes. In the parlor, she gently touched the woodwork on the mantle, wood that was probably walnut, tightly fitted by the master carpenter. "My papa, he did this," she said softly. She went into the bedroom and looked at built-in cabinets, a cupboard, a closet, and she said, "My papa, he did this, too, ain't it beautiful?" Jody Grimes asked Mrs. Gibbs if the people in the neighborhood knew this was the childhood home of Babe Didrikson and she replied, "We didn't know it was her home until a year or two after we moved in. I have made certain that my children are aware of it, that they are living in a historic place. But I have my doubts whether many people in the neighborhood are aware of it."

There was reassuring solidarity in the house, perfectly fit joints, heavy beams, tight window frames. Lillie wandered about and touched the walls, the door frames, the windowpanes. She said, "Oh, my, I feel that they're still here – Papa and Babe and my mama." She wandered into the kitchen and out onto the large enclosed porch that was Ole Didriksen's pride. "Oh, how this used to be so fulla fresh air. Yes, they was sixteen windows. Here's where we washed dishes. And Babe used to have to scrub this floor, I remember. Oh, that Babe, she'd put on the scrub brushes like skates, tie 'em right to her feet, and scrub the floor, whistlin' around like some ballet dancer on ice skates." The porch was neither sunny nor particularly full of fresh air. No one had skated on scrub brushes in a long time. There were crates, cardboard boxes, broken toys stored there, the windows were shut tight, all of them. Mrs. Gibbs apologized further for the look of the place. Lillie pointed to a section of the porch and said, "Papa slept right there and he could snore to his heart's content ever' night."

A steep flight of stairs led up from the porch to the second floor. Lillie climbed sighing. "This here was the apartment Papa built for me and Babe after she came back from the Olympics. Yeah, we lived up here for a while." She went to the front window and looked out. "Oh, yeah, I remember many's the day and night I'd sit up here and peek out at Obie. He lived right there across the street from us, and, oh, I really had a crush on him. I never thought I'd marry him. Now Obie's gone, too, ain't he." The apartment upstairs consisted of two small rooms, one at the front, one at the back, a tiny hallway and a bathroom. The bathroom contained a large bright green bathtub, sink and commode, and Lillie peeked in and chuckled. "This is Babe's Hollywood bathroom. She seen how the stars lived when she was in Los Angeles and she always wanted what she called her Hollywood bathroom. Oh, this was the most beautiful bathroom in Beaumont."

Lillie descended the stairs and went into the backyard. A huge sycamore tree stood there. "That's where we swung and played circus," she said, "and over there, Papa had a little place where he worked on fixin' antique furniture for the rich people." The yard was strewn with things. A rusty bedspring lay half in, half out of a garage. There were a couple of old tires on the ground. Lillie thanked Mrs. Gibbs, and left in Jody's car. She was pleased with having seen the old home and she spoke excitedly, "Oh, my, did you see Babe's Hollywood bathroom? Did you see my papa's porch? Oh, my, oh my." The car rolled slowly up Doucette Avenue; Lillie pointed out old landmarks. "That's where Magnolia School was, where Babe won the marble contest." The schoolyard was an empty lot, weedy and rocky with a "For Sale" sign at one corner. "There's the bakery we used to get our birthday cakes at. There's the shoe place, same as it was when we lived here. Is the same man there now? I don't know, I don't know." Toward the end of the street, at the corners where Doucette dead-ends at a chain-mail fence surrounding the oil refinery, Lillie pointed at a small building, its windows boarded, its door padlocked. "That's the dive where Papa drank beer. He'd dance there and have a real good time. Sometime he'd get drunk as a jackass. I remember I had to go up there and bring him home for supper some nights. Papa liked beer, yes, he did."

She asked Jody to drive back to 850 Doucette. They parked the car and Lillie sat looking at the shabby old house. "Ain't that a beautiful place," she said. There was still music in the house. It was nothing like the Stephen Foster songs the Didriksens used to love. From inside the house came the sound of a piano; Mrs. Gibb's nephew was playing Debussy's "Claire de Lune."

Lillie spoke sadly: "Life changes, don't it. Dora died a few years ago out in Arizona. She and her husband lived in a shack; he was a prospector. Esther's in California, but she won't talk to none of us. She couldn't get along with Babe. She wanted to be a movie star and she never went out in the sun. Then Ole, the oldest, he's here in Beaumont, but he don't like to talk about Babe and he kind of likes to be by himself. Louis is over in Newton and he's got a nice business. We get along. Bubba, he's never here. Bubba, he's in the oil. He lives in – what's that country? – he lives over in Libya. The family got broke up and spread around. I feel so bad sometimes."

Chapter
4

After Babe Didrikson became a national heroine at the Tenth Olympiad, she was often interviewed by journalists who pressed her to reveal the secret of her success. In one "inside story" she spoke at length about this:

People think it is a little strange that I do not seem to be worried or nervous before I run a race. Why should I be that way? I'm only running against girls. If there were some of the boys that I was brought up with back in Beaumont that was just as liable to pull a trip on me any time I was stepping out in front as be doing something nice and refined, well, maybe I would be a little skittish. So I don't worry about the races with girls. Now, don't get me wrong there, mister, I don't mean that these girls are not great runners and that they haven't courage. What I mean is that I have the advantage over them because I grew up competing against wiry, tough boys and that gave me experience that most of the girl runners today never had.

The way I look at it a girl that wants to become an athlete and do some winning should get that kind of a start by being a tomboy. If she just goes in for games against girls when she is young, why she never gets used to being smashed around. Girls are nice to each other. Boys are rough with each other, and rougher with girls who crash into their game.

I have been asked if I could give advice to girls on how to be better athletes, but I am afraid that the only real first class advice I can give is get toughened up playing the boys' games, but DON'T GET TOUGH. There's a lot of difference there.

Whether she was "tough" or merely "toughened" Babe did cut a hard-knuckled swathe through Beaumont's South End. She was a fighter, endlessly daring other children to step across lines drawn in the playground dirt, punching arms to "make a knot," kicking, tripping, pulling hair. Her homeroom teacher in junior high school recalled: "I called her Babe, but I always had the feeling she wanted me to call her Mildred. I remember the boys in my room continually teased Mildred, thumped and hit her when going through the halls. But that girl had a way of getting even out on the grounds. She would step on their heels and kick them. They didn't make anything off Mildred."

Once, when she was a freshman in high school, a strapping football player named Red Reynolds stuck out his chin and told Babe that he doubted she'd be able to hurt him, no matter what she did. She swung once, hit him on the chin and he dropped to the floor, senseless. For years, Red Reynolds bragged about how he had once been dropped by the famous Babe Didrikson.

Belligerence was an intrinsic part of her personality as a youngster. She was constantly ready to turn to violence if she was crossed; she was evidently a fierce little racist too, according to people who knew her then. This was a common attitude among Southern white people of lower-class upbringing, but Babe backed up her racism with her fists. There are countless stories of Babe coming in late for school, her knuckles bruised, her face cut or lumpy, and when she was asked what had happened, time after time her schoolmates and teachers heard some version of this quote: "Oh, some niggers wouldn't get out of my way and I had to cold-cock 'em." A former Beaumont physical education teacher who knew Babe well then, said: "She really did hate blacks in those days. I think she went out of her way to antagonize them and, truly, to *hurt* them. I don't know what the genesis of this might have been, probably it had a lot to do with the tough neighborhood she lived in."

The dead-end nature of Beaumont's South End had a great deal to do with forming the stubborn temperament and nourishing the physical talent of the woman who would become the best athlete of her sex. One of her best friends – and a constant opponent – in the South End was Raymond Alford, a barefoot and ragged little towhead who grew up to be a sports hero at Beaumont High School, later to be the athletic director of the local school system for more than thirty-five years. In 1975, Raymond Alford was sixty-seven, retired from his school career, a handsome fellow with a full head of flaxen white hair. He was tanned, fit, full of courtly goodwill. He said, "Babe made the statement in her book that I was her high school hero. But there was no courtship, no love interest, no sir. She didn't give a hang about boys – we were only good for playing sports with or to whip up on. I moved on to Doucette in nineteen twenty-one or twenty-two. My papa was a sawmill man, he followed the sawmill trail and the family had kept moving to wherever there was wood to be cut. Finally my mama told my daddy that the children had to have regular schools and a regular church and she was takin' us to Beaumont. We were barefoot all the time. All of us in the South End were poor. Not on welfare, but darn poor.

"I got acquainted with Babe first on the sandlots on Saturdays. You know how kids get together. All the boys in the neighborhood'd come and Babe was *always* there. Let me tell you, she was the only girl, but she was also among the first to be chosen. She was not just hanging around till the last, no sir. We played on an old vacant lot at the streetcar barn on Doucette. We kept it up ourselves, cut the grass, drew the baselines. Ordinarily we didn't have anything to do with girls then. Babe was different. Once you saw her play, you didn't mind having her around. At first we might have put her in right field, like you always did the worst and weakest ones, but not for long. She was playing shortstop or third base, although I don't recall her ever pitching for us.

"She had a temper. She wanted to excel. She wanted to show you up. I don't know if that was because she was against *men* or against feminine things or what. She was not what you'd call unfeminine. But she did not care a hang about makeup or fussy clothing. When we talked, we'd talk about athletes. We played against each other all the time. If she beat me, I could never make myself congratulate her. I'd just say, 'I'll practice some more, Babe, and I'll getcha next time.' "

Raymond Alford was a star of the football team; the coach was a typically supercharged Texas football booster named Lilburn "Bubba" Dimmitt. Alford recalled, "I was the kicker on the team, but one time Babe went up to Coach Dimmitt and told him that I wasn't good enough at kicking extra points and that she could do lots better. Here she was, just this li'l bitty thing, out there on the field, jawin' with coach, saying, 'I can beat Raymond all to little bits and pieces at kicking. You got to let me come out and kick those points for you, Bubba.' Well, Bubba Dimmitt liked Babe and he let her try and kick some. And, you know, she was better 'n I was – *lots* better. Bubba really wanted to let Babe try it, but there was no way the school board would let her in the games. The Texas league rules were flat against letting a girl play a man's sport. Babe's poor old heart was broken, but there was nothing to be done."

Raymond Alford spoke about Babe's motivation to succeed, the intensity of her determination to excel: "I think her motives were probably a lot like mine. I knew that winning in sports was the only way I'd ever be recognized. Babe and I were both from poor families. If you did not have a car or if you did not have money, you were unacceptable. I thought that I might get to be the same as the richer people if I were good at sports; I figured I'd be asked to their parties. Sports was a way of getting to be equal, and I think that's what carried Babe through and made her work so hard. It was the same as with the blacks in the fifties and sixties. There was no other way to get ahead except sports. I remember the dances at the high school; the people who could go, they had cars and nice suits to wear. I didn't, but if I was an athlete I could hobnob with 'em. That was my motivation. I think it was Babe's too. She was just as poor as I was."

Babe's career at Beaumont High School was a single-minded, one-faceted affair: she did almost nothing but sports. This placed her in a tiny minority of girls, a group considered rather odd. Ruth Scurlock said: "There was an academic group and an athletic group among the girls. Babe and her few friends in the athletic group wore denim skirts with pockets, socks like gym hose and flat oxford shoes. The others, the so-called society girls, wore their hair permanent waved. They wore silk stockings and high heels. These were the 'sissy girls' to Babe. These were frothy girls and they were not useful in Babe's eyes, but they were in the overwhelming majority and they were the leaders. It was terribly difficult for Babe to do what she wanted to do. Even in her own tough neighborhood, the other girls didn't like her because she was an athlete. Her very excellence at sports made her unacceptable to other girls. She was an alien in her own land, believe me."

Babe's photograph appeared several times in the *Pine Burr,* the Beaumont High School yearbook, in the editions of 1928, 1929 and 1930. She was on every girls' team – volleyball, tennis, golf, baseball, basketball, swimming. In every photograph she was frowning, squinting suspiciously at the camera, a dead-end kid with straight hair and severe bangs. In 1928, the schoolboy editors of the *Pine Burr* wrote about her skills as a basketball player in glowing terms: "Babe is her nickname and although just that in experience she is far from that in ability. She plays with an ease and grace rivalling that of a dancer to tally goal after goal for the Purple during the season." In 1929 the editors wrote: "Babe has been a very necessary player on the Miss Royal Purple squad this year. She never failed to star in any game, at home or abroad. She is a very capable forward who very seldom misses the basket. When 'Babe' gets the ball, the scorekeeper gets his adding machine, and then he sometimes loses count." In 1930, the year she dropped out of school to join the Casualty Insurance Company's Golden Cyclones in Dallas, they wrote: "Toward the end of the year when the unit of the machine was working with machinelike accuracy, Babe Didrikson, one of the main cogs, was withdrawn."

She excelled, but she was not popular. She was an aberration, in her way, a living put-down to all things feminine. Her female classmates were excited about their first lipsticks, jewelry, girdles and bobby pins, about their first brassieres, about patent leather high heels. Babe abhorred these things. Tiny Scurlock, the *Journal* sports editor, recalled that Babe's mother once told him: "Babe wanted to go to a party one night, so I made her a very pretty dress with lace around the collar and frills around the bottom of the skirt. When I called her in and showed her the dress and told her she could go to the party, I thought she'd have a fit. Did she like it? I should say not. I finally got it on her, but would you believe it, when she looked in the mirror she tore it off and put on her overalls and struck out for the party." Tiny also reported in his biography of Babe: "Around Doucette Avenue, she favored knickers, blouses, overalls, boys pants, athletic underwear and undershirts. At home, she slept in her brothers' union suits."

She must have looked like some kind of female Huckleberry Finn, raffish and pugnacious, compared to the preening child-women of Beaumont. In those days, the ultimate model high school maiden was a powdered, docile trinket, pretty yet weak, beholden for favors, for support, for survival even to young men (athletes preferred, if you please). Ideal women were ornaments. The Miss America Pageant had begun as an obscure resort promotion in 1921 with eight contestants; it immediately became so popular that in 1924 eighty-three young women entered, and Miss America was one of the most admired, the most envied people in the country, even though she clearly had almost nothing to bring to the world except good looks. Beaumont High School was no different: zest, strength, speed, even intelligence in women counted for far less than good looks. Within the social structure of the school, there was no greater honor for a girl than to be elected a Sponsor of a sports team. She was required merely to be pretty and rather obsequious. The *Pine Burr* of 1930 described the Football Sponsor and her Court of Maids this way:

As in the olden days of chivalry, the "faire ladye", graciously acknowledged queen, smiled upon her lord in knightly combat, inspiring him to victory. Thus did our fair Sponsor and Maids aid the Royal Purple football team. By their faith in them and their sincere enthusiasm, they encouraged the boys to victory, but they never let their zeal detract from their fairness or good sportsmanship. Those seven girls have attended practice daily and injected the sort of fight in those boys which brings forth their best efforts.

Perhaps it is significant that such sweet and mealy language can no longer be found in America today except for one place: captions on the Playmate layouts in *Playboy* magazine.

Though sports Sponsors were considered elite as individuals, the organization in Beaumont High School that most young women considered *the* most select group of all was something called The Kacklers Club. The *Pine Burr* editors wrote about the club in this fashion: " 'Athletes are our favorite boys.' This will provide the key note as to the origin and purpose of the Kacklers. The real aim of this club is to provide adequate entertainment for our athletes, and to do everything possible to the furtherance of sportsmanlike athletic activities. There is a spirit of sisterly love and unity that only a Kackler can have. This is an organization of dignity, and naturally its members have gained the respect and honor of everyone." Such feckless hooey probably made Babe Didrikson nauseous. Yet this role of demure and passive sideline princesses was the norm for young ladies in those days. Ruth Scurlock said: "Babe was bucking society even then. She was simply being herself. She really had no other choice, I suppose. It certainly must have been painfully difficult at times."

If Babe was a social pariah in school, she was clearly a paragon of sport. Her physical education teacher was a small sinewy woman named Beatrice Lytle, who was then in her twenties. It was her first job as a teacher but she pioneered a surprisingly diverse sports program for girls. In 1975 Bea Lytle was seventy-five, retired from her job in the Houston physical education department (she had left Beaumont in the early 1930s). She had spent fifty years in physical education. She said, "I saw possibly twelve thousand young women over those years. I observed them closely and I trained a lot of them to be fine athletes. But there was never anyone in all those thousands who was anything like Babe. I never again saw the likes of her. Babe was blessed with a body that was perfect. I can still remember how her muscles *flowed* when she walked. She had a neuromuscular coordination that is very, very rare."

Beatrice Lytle gave Babe her first formal training in a variety of sports. She recalled, "Babe was the most teachable person I have ever known. You could explain the rudiments of a golf swing, a basketball movement, and Babe could do it. I showed Babe her first golf club around nineteen twenty-seven, I guess. She would caddy for me on Saturdays at the municipal course. It was a horrible place, full of snakes. The greens were made of sand. Babe took to the game very well, although it was all quite rudimentary. Those stories about her driving the ball two hundred and fifty yards the first time she swung a club or about shooting in the nineties her first round — they are just stories, they are not true. She could outdrive me after a while, it is true, but she never did beat me on the Beaumont course." Bea Lytle kept the first set of golf clubs Babe Didrikson ever used. They hung on the wall of her garage in Houston, the clubheads darkened and nicked from use. Miss Lytle said, "I have kept them because I think they have historic value. I hope someday there will be a museum to send them to."

Though golf was the game Babe was best known for in her later years, it was not important to her in Beaumont. The sport she excelled at was basketball. In the 1920s, this was the premier women's team sport in the United States and large crowds turned out to watch high school girls play. Certain prudes, including many members of the Women's Division, were convinced the real attraction for male spectators was the sight of all those young women cavorting in bloomers; but in fact women's basketball was a fast, exciting game. Babe was an aggressive, sharp-elbowed player. She was high scorer and sparkplug of her team, which was called the Miss Royal Purples. The team never lost a game when she played. Her favorite teammate was Lois "Pee Wee" Blanchette, a retired physical education teacher who in 1975 still lived in Beaumont and still reflected a certain feisty sense of rivalry with Babe. "Tiny never gave her any more write-ups than he gave me, you know," said Pee Wee. "I was her running mate. Oh, I never scored like she did because I was a running and passing forward and she was the shooting forward. I always wanted to be just as great as Babe. In basketball I think I was, yes, I do. But I couldn't *ever* fight like she, I couldn't be as tough. And it wasn't my fault I didn't score so much. I wasn't the shooting forward, I was the *hustling* forward and I fed the ball to Babe, I fed her *perfectly*. One game, I decided I wanted to make one basket, just one. Babe threw me a pass. It was way behind me. I couldn't get a shot at *all*. I was so disgusted I threw that ball up in the air. The crowd went crazy. They loved me for that. We were a terrific team. The boys wouldn't admit it, but they liked the girls' team to play the same nights as they did because we brought such big crowds. The Miss Royal Purples didn't know what losing was, we never believed we'd ever lose. And we never did.

"Babe never let up when she played sports. She put it all out, I know that. Except this one time I remember. She and I, we were playing doubles in a tennis tournament in Beaumont. It was after she got back from winnin' the Olympics and being so famous. She and I were playing together. Well, that girl, she was just goofin' off and *blowin'* the game. I stepped up and stopped the play and I went over to Babe. 'Hey!' I said. 'You got all those medals at the Olympic Games and ever'one in the world *knows* your name and here all I want is this li'l ol' bitty tiny cup and *you* won't even help me get it. *C'mon,* Babe!' Well, sure enough, Babe pulled herself together and buckled down and we won me my cup. I'll never forget that."

For Pee Wee Blanchette, sport was only a passing sometime thing. "I knew from when I was an ittty-bitty girl that I wanted to be a teacher," she said. "I took my studies seriously because of this. But Babe, well, she never had ideas like that about herself. She was sports, nothing but sports. Babe never had any choice but to be a great athlete. She had no other way to go."

Babe's physical education teacher, Bea Lytle, agreed: "She had very poor grades most of the way through school. Sometimes she only passed the minimum three courses, just enough to stay eligible for sports. Babe *had* to succeed as an athlete. Her physical equipment was so much better than her mental equipment at the time. She never had a vision of herself as being anything but an athlete. She simply did not know any other vision." Ruth Scurlock said: "I have no doubt that Babe had the best IQ of anyone in the Didriksen family, but I don't think in her whole life she ever read a book unless it had the rules of some game in it."

In a sense, the world's greatest woman athlete was as much a product of her intellectual limitations as she was of her prodigious physical talent. To excel as she did at sports required a single-mindedness, a *narrow*-mindedness, which allowed no other possibilities in life to intrude. Her sister Lillie recalled: "Babe just did what she had to do, she went out and become a great famous athlete. She never once *said* she was gonna do that, she just done it. She never thought at all."

Had Babe had a more speculative turn of mind, had she been more imaginative, she might well have abandoned sports as a way of life long before she succeeded at it. Had she been more sensitive to the hostility around her, to the climate of negativism toward women's sports, she might not have tried at all. But she was dealing in instinct rather than intellect, and she could only do what was natural for her. Fortunately, she was soon taken out of the unproductive environment of Beaumont. She left behind the gunnysack-factory future that the South End seemed to promise, and she escaped the unfriendly high school world that was dominated by the Kacklers. She began a two-and-a-half-year period that changed her completely. She went into it as a tough little high school girl who was good at games and she emerged as the phenomenon known as Whatta Gal.

Chapter
5

On a rainy night in Houston in the winter of 1930, a tall pallid fellow named Melvin Jackson McCombs entered the life of Babe Didrikson. He was plainly a man of means; he wore a dove-gray Stetson on his graying hair, a thick tweed suit with a vest and a heavy plaid overcoat with a tie-around belt. He had a dignified mien and people called him "Colonel" because he had once been in the army. At the time he met Babe, Colonel McCombs was manager of the department of safety for the Employers Casualty Company. That meant he headed the division that specialized in accident and cyclone insurance for farmers and ranchers in the Southwest. Safety Department Manager may have been his title, but his major preoccupation with the company was to manage its athletic teams for women – basketball, softball, track and field. Because of the kind of insurance McComb's department handled and because the company's athletes worked for him, the teams were called the Golden Cyclones.

On this wet night in 1930, Colonel McCombs attended a basketball game between Babe's Beaumont High School team and one from Houston; he was scouting the teams for recruits, and he was there specifically to see not Babe, but the star of the Houston team. When he saw Babe play, the Colonel ignored the other girl. He hurried to the Beaumont locker room where he urged Babe to quit high school, go to work for Employers Casualty and play for the Golden Cyclones. The Colonel was a persuasive fellow. He offered her a job as a stenographer in his safety department; the pay was to be seventy-five dollars a month. He warned her that she was still a minor, however, and that she would need her parents' permission if she wished to take the job. In reality Colonel McCombs was offering Babe an opportunity to be a basketball player on a semiprofessional basis. There were dozens of such women's teams around the country, though they were strongest in the Midwest and South. Industrial basketball for women was a popular and powerful sport. For men, college basketball was the primary outlet for the game, but few colleges had strong programs for women. Thus, teams run by corporations or churches offered the only real chance for women to play in top-level competition. They were exploitative in that the teams were essentially an arm of a firm's drive for good public relations (a term that had not yet been invented in the 1930s) but there was no other serious basketball for women.

For a girl with Babe's passion for athletics (plus her low esteem for anything academic), the Golden Cyclones offered a remarkable and timely opportunity. Nevertheless, Babe received the offer from the Colonel with at least superficial aplomb. A teammate, Thelma Hughes, who was with her in Houston that night, recalled: "Here she had just got this big offer from Colonel McCombs to move to Dallas and play for the Golden Cyclones – we *all* knew about them. The rest of us were all excited. But after the game, up in our rooms in the Rice Hotel, Babe didn't seem to be thinking about the offer. She was too busy leaning out the window trying to see how many people she could spit at and hit on the head when they walked below on the sidewalk."

At home in Beaumont, the Didriksens were at first bewildered by the offer, and they were skeptical. They debated at length whether their daughter should be allowed to drop out of school – even for such good money. (The salary came to $900 a year; in 1930, an average typist got $624, a coal miner $723). Lillie Grimes recalled her parents' discussion: "My mama and papa thought and thought about Babe's goin' over to Dallas. She wanted to go in the *worst* way, but she seemed so young, you know. Finally, Papa made up his mind. He put down his pipe and said, "Goddommitt' – that's the way Papa talked – *'Goddommit!* you *go!"* He decided that's what they all came from Norway *for* – to give the kids everything they could in America. Babe, she promised to come back often and see my mama, but Mama, she just hated to see her baby go. She'd pretend to smile and be her happy ol' self, but she wasn't. She'd be in the kitchen bakin' bread and her face'd be red and twisted and then I'd see a teardrop fall in the bread pan. My mama she hated to see Babe go to Dallas." Babe left high school on February 17, 1930, and she played her first game for the Golden Cyclones on February 18. The next day she wrote the first of a remarkably revealing series of letters to her friend Tiny Scurlock at the Beaumont *Journal.* Tiny kept this correspondence squirreled away in his collection of memorabilia and newspaper clippings about Babe. In the course of the thirty-plus months covered by these letters, it is possible to see clearly Babe's transformation from a star-struck teenage tomboy to the swaggering young woman who became an Olympic heroine in Los Angeles.

The first letter was written in a vigorous childlike scrawl and her exuberance shone as brightly as her innocence. "Dear Tiny: Played my first game last nigh [*sic*] the 18, and I never before practice with them and they say that I was the the [*sic*] girl that that [*sic*] they have been looking for. They put me to start and kept me in until the finish. Tiny I am a working girl and have got to get busy. Please keep this write up for me please or send it back when you get a chance. Thanks so much, Babe." She included a clipping indicating that the Golden Cyclones won 48–18 and that she scored fourteen points.

Two days later she excitedly scrawled another letter: "Dear 'Tiny' – The games are coming in pretty fast here lately. We played Seagoville again last night and tomorrow at Cisco, Texas, and Monday night we play the champs of city. They have beaten the Cyclones but if I can help it they wont do it anymore. I am sending two write ups & me box score. they don't give you any write ups here. Well Good by Babe P.S. Please save write up for me." She enclosed a clipping indicating the Golden Cyclones won 46–15 and she had scored sixteen points.

Life was beautiful. Babe had entered a universe that might have been made of her own dreams: she was in an environment where swift muscular athletic women were the norm rather than an aberration. She was not ostracized but lionized for her dedication to sports. Although she worked regular hours at her stenography job, her major pursuit for Employers Casualty was as an athlete. The company was anxious to wring a maximum amount of publicity out of its women's sports program. This meant the team had to win and, thus, the firm endowed the Golden Cyclones with first-class equipment, excellent coaching, flamboyant uniforms of bright yellow or orange, and plenty of time to practice.

On March 6, 1930, Babe sent Tiny a letter she had typed. It was virtually without an error (she had once won a typing contest in high school, averaging eighty-six words a minute). She wrote:

Dear "Tiny" – Boy I am still knocking them cold, we started in the S.A.A.U. [Southern Amateur Athletic Union] tournament this week and are stilling holding out very fine and hope we keep on. We played the Western Union Tuesday night and beat them 62 to 9 and we played the Evary team last night and we beat them 82 to 5 [an enclosed box score showed Didrikson with thirty-six points in this game]. We have two All American guards and two All American forwards on our team and Mr. McCombs said that he would have three All American Forwards and Three All American Guards before the season is over. So Tiny I am up here now and that is what I am going to be, just watch and see. I will be home I guess about April the 3rd or the 5th somewheres around there, that is after the National A.A.U. is over and I get that All American Badge to put on my left sleeve of this hot orange sweater that I have. "Tiny" – I have had two more offers and they are from the Sun Oil and the Sparkman of Ark. The Oil Man said that he could use me in the national this year but I am going to stay with the Golden Cyclones until this season is over, we have a new coach and our playing is 100% better. "Tiny" How was the picture and what have you done with it. maybe in the national I will be able to send to Beaumont a picture of me in the news paper about the national A.A.U. Hope so anyhow. Well to be frank with you I am going to make an All American cause I have got my mind set on that. Well Tiny I have to close. Good by. Babe.

She had been with the Golden Cyclones less than three weeks and already she was attracting corporate recruiters trying to steal her for their own teams. She was now suddenly aware that she had value as a commodity and that her value in this market could be increased through publicity. On March 19, 1930, one month after she left Beaumont, she wrote:

Dearest tiny – Have gotten a lot of write ups from all of the leading news papers in the South. And I surely do thank you for giving me the publicity and I surely did need it. because when I came over here, I didn't know any one. I have a whole lots of fans now. and they are all going for the "Golden Cyclones" and betting on them. I am leaving Saturday for Wichita Kansas where I am going to enter national

A.A.U. Tournament. Tiny – they have entered me for the Golden Cyclones to be in the free shot tournament because I won it over here in Dallas. I made a new record of 57 out of 65 shots. I see that the St. Anthony team had beaten the Royal Purple. to bad I surely do hate that. well Tiny tell everyone you see hello for me   Babe

Sister Lillie accompanied Babe to the national A.A.U. championships in Wichita that winter. They were still a clumsy pair of bumpkin children. They took a train from Dallas to Wichita and Lillie recalled the trip: "We was afraid to leave the train when it stopped 'cuz we were afraid it'd leave us behind. Oh, we was so silly. My mama, she had told us when we went to bed on the train, we *had* to be sure to wash our underwear. We washed it in a little bitty sink and we hung it out the window to dry overnight. When we woke up, our underwear was black as soot and we had to do it all over again and then wear it wet. Oh, my."

In Wichita the Golden Cyclones swept through to the finals, then lost to Sun Oil (a team that had been trying to steal Babe) by one point. She scored two hundred and ten points in five games and was chosen an All-American forward. The tournament was a splendid showplace for her skills. Packs of corporate sport wolves were after her now. On May 9, 1930, she received one fascinating letter from the company recruiter of the Kansas City Life Insurance Company. It was addressed to "Miss Babe Dedrickson, c/o Employer Indemnity Ins. Co., Girls Basketball Team, Dallas, Tex." It said: "Dear Miss Dedrickson: Would you be interested in a position with the Kansas City Life Insurance Company of Kansas City, Mo.? That company has had a mediocre girls basketball team for the last three or four years and is now interested in having a real team to compete for the national championship and has advised me to get in touch with some of the leading players in this section of the country." The writer, R. C. Martin, the team coach, said that the company had a gymnasium in its home office building, that there was a surplus of job applications on file "but girls playing basketball will be given preference," that Babe would be paid $80 a month to start and given "free medical attention." Beyond that, basketball players were given an extra inducement to win: "We will pay a bonus for overtime work $25.00 per victory in regular games," wrote Martin, "$50.00 per victory in city tournament games, $100.00 per victory in national tournament games, with an additional $100.00 for winning the local cup, $100.00 additional for winning of city championship, and an additional bonus in accordance with those others if the team should win the national tournament. This bonus is divided among the players." The recruiter told Babe that she should apply for a job – any job: "such as filing, clerking, typing, etc. If you have had no experience do not hesitate to say so as that will have no bearing on your opportunity."

Babe was at this point negotiating a contract with Tiny Scurlock to be her manager and she sent the Kansas City Life offer to him. However, she was not really interested in thinking about her basketball career now: she had just been introduced to a challenging new world – track and field. Babe had never tried this sport before; Colonel McCombs had her do the javelin, the baseball throw, the shot put, the high jump and the long jump. She was an instant phenomenon. On May 21, 1930, she typed another letter:

Dearest Tiny – Have been very busy with track, and track meet that we had Saturday at S.M.U. [Southern Methodist University]. Our team won plenty easy with about 48 points to the good. The reason why I haven't written to you is because I have had nothing to say, we have been out every evening for track practice and are going out again.

I am the track captain, we elected right after the meet at S.M.U. Saturday. I am enclosing the write ups that they gave us in the paper. So that you can see how everything came out. Next Sunday Kate Carriager and myself are going to practice for Tennis doubles and gonna take everything. We have played base ball three times and won all three games. we played Davis Hat Company yesterday and beat them 26 to 4. easy game. Boy Tiny if I hadn't sat down on that last broad jump I could have broken the world's record just like taking candy from a baby. But next Saturday the 31th and I am gonna break a record in every thing that I go out for. Last Saturday I entered four things and won first in all four. In about three or four days Jacoby will give us our medals. That is four to the string that I am heading for. Well, by and get that thing ready so that I can see it [referring to the contract between them], I don't think so much about that letter [the Kansas City offer] do you? Until next time. Babe Didrikson.

Her signature had taken on a new flamboyance, it had the quality of an autograph. On June 8, she typed another letter:

Dear tiny. – Just got back from Shreveport from the Southern Track meet. Well that makes the 13th gold medal that I have gotten. Made me a bracelet out of the first ten that I got and I got 3 from the Southern Meet. All gold and no silver. I am sending you a write up from the Times.

Why don't you drop me a line once in a while and tell me about what you are going to do. Well Tiny I have got to go out to the track field at S.M.U. and brush up for the Texas and the National meet. So that I can Break a few worlds records.

I am going to enter the tennis, swimming and every other kind of meet over here and over there. get full of medals. You know like ants.

Some typest Huh? Just Babe. Babe.

Her letters were like a combination of battlefield reports from a remarkably victorious general and merry postcards from a child at camp. On June 23, 1930 (three days before her nineteenth birthday), Babe wrote in a quick, excited scribble:

Dear Tiny. Had the Texas A.A.U. Track Meet Saturday. We have had 4 track meets so far. and Tiny I have made first place in all four of them and have been high pointer in all. I have a record in every meet and every thing that I have. Boy! I surely did cut my foot. I was just going out for practice Thursday and the bathhouse had a broken bottle all over the floor and of course I would step on the biggest piece. I went to the Doctor 2 times and he gouged around and made it so sore. but boy did i jump. And throw that Ball & Javelin, put that shot. Just read these write ups and see. High Jump ½ inch below the World record. My team has won all the meets so far. The National meet will be a fight between Chicago and Cyclones of Dallas. Mr. McCombs has us guessed winning by six points. Mighty good guesser, has guessed every meet and wasn't 1 point less on all but one and perfect on it – 70 and our score was 70. Well Tiny how about a nice write up over there in Beaumont. remember the scrape book is almost full. Oh! yeah! Right after the Track season I am gonna train for the Olympic in 1932 on the Broad Jump, High Jump true Western roll. Baseball and Javelin Throw. Train 2 times a week into 1932. Practice makes perfect. Boy at the National & Olympic gonna show everyone I have ants in my pants. By – Babe – P.S. Please send these write ups to my mama. have gotten 18 gold medals and no silver or bronze Thanks – Babe. And the rest you have of me put them in my scrape book. Babe.

Babe was so full of herself in these months. Her "scrape book" of newspaper clippings was attended with the same ecstatic care as another girl might handle love letters from a particularly exciting beau. She simply could not fail at anything she tried. On July 7, 1930, she wrote:

Dear Tiny! Here is where I ought to get a big write up in the Beaumont. Tiny I was one of six girls from America to go to Germany next August 1930 and Tiny Mr. Bingham President of the National A.A.U. and all of the officials said that I had a berth on the Olympic team in the 1932 without a doubt. Tiny fix me up a good write up. I will send you a brief scetch. I have broken 6 American records, 7 or 8 Southern records and 4 world records. I broke three world records in the national the 4th [of July]. I broke the Javelin which was 129 feet and I threw it 133 feet 6½ inches. New world record official baseball which was 258 feet I broke it by 268 feet. And broke it in an exhibition 274 feet and Tiny you know Stella Walsh . . . beat me in the broad jump. We both broke the world's record. My first jump I fouled. I jumped 18 feet 11½ inches, but the foul didn't count. My second jump was 18 feet 8¾ in and hers was 18 feet 9⅛ inches. Tough luck. The old world record is 18 feet 7½ inches. Well Tiny I get a vacation pretty soon and I guess I will come home for about 4 or 5 days. And then I will tell you about the trip to Germany. Yours for a big headline. Babe.

The trip to Germany did not occur, but the Golden Cyclones had finished second in the 1930 A.A.U. track and field meet. Babe was the star. At the end of her first season as a track and field competitor, she held national records in the javelin, the baseball throw, and Southern A.A.U. records in the high jump, the eight-pound shot put and the long jump.

The first year with the Golden Cyclones was a skyrocket ride to success. Babe was launched to the highest American levels of competition in basketball and track and field, and she excelled. It would be hard to imagine a more sensational debut and the following season had to be a comedown, if for no other reason than that the novelty of such heady conquest would be missing. The basketball team was even more successful than the year before, winning the A.A.U.

national championship this time. Babe scored one hundred and ninety-five points in six games and, once more, she was selected an All American. But the first year of innocent, endless joy in victory was indeed behind her. Babe was different and her relationship with her mentor McCombs was changed, too. A new note of connivance entered her correspondence, and in the spring of 1931 she tried to enlist Scurlock in a scheme to squeeze more money out of the insurance company:

Dearest "Tiny" Why hello old top, how in the heck are you getting along. Now this is the time that I need a manager. Tiny I think that I should be making more money so I am asking you to write me a letter telling me of a better job that I can get and more money – about $125.00 a month, you see they have us under a twelve month rule, that is if you played in the national tournament with one team you can't change clubs until one year after the date of the last game that you played with this one team. So if you will tell me its a better job as professional and more money. You know kinda shake 'em up a little.

They wouldn't want to let me go for nothing.

Colonel McCombs made that twelve month rule so that he could keep us in the Co. and make us work for nothing. But he has another think coming. I know good and well I am worth $150.00 and I am gonna get it out of this company, with your help.

All I want is a letter from you telling me all about a keen proposition that you have found for me. And kinda stretch it, see, cause when I show it to him he will raise my pay to about what you say in that offer. This is just to make them break loose and pay me a little more dough.

Put the price and everything. Make a keen contract form, and make it plenty real – 'C.' Tiny don't tell anyone about this will you, because I couldn't have it get to Dallas –

The president is giving me free Golf Lessons out at Dallas Country Club, and they are plenty nice so they won't have to raise my pay. When I get your letter I will take it in to Mr. McCombs and show it to him. I am the only prospect of him winning the National and he knows that, plenty of teams want me, but can't get me on account of the 12 months rule. The only way out is to turn Professional and that will make them chirp up and pay me what they ought to. All the rest of the teams get payed keen and lots more than any of us do. So Tiny will you please do that for me. Write just as though I had never written to you – so they won't suspect. Love Babe Didrikson.

No one living in 1975 remembered Tiny Scurlock or Babe mentioning this letter or this scheme. Tiny Scurlock's files contained this letter, but no further reference to it. Apparently nothing was done. Her next letter to Tiny, four weeks later, on May 25, 1931, made no mention of it.:

Dear Tiny Haven't kept in touch with you lately but have a pretty good write up that I think you would like to run in the paper. You see I am playing on the men's baseball team now. And will get good write ups right along for that. And I think that you can get a Dallas paper, the paper who carry my stories are the Times Herald, The Dallas Journal & Dispatch. I am gonna pitch first three innings then go to right field. Well see you in about two months. Your friend Babe Didrikson.

That summer Babe excelled at track and field. The national A.A.U. meet was held in Jersey City, New Jersey. The Golden Cyclones were the runner-up team once more, with nineteen points. Babe got fifteen points by winning the baseball throw, the 80-meter hurdles and the broad jump. Early in August 1931, the Dallas *Morning News* ran a half-page photo montage of Babe, "ace of the local Golden Cyclones," and declared that she was probably "the world's outstanding all round feminine athlete."

It was only nineteen months since she had left the trolley barn lot games on Doucette Avenue and now she was attracting headlines as the best in the world. It was a heavy burden for an unsophisticated, uneducated young woman to carry and Babe did not do it very well. She became more arrogant, more self-centered than before. She also began to act more mannish, more hard-boiled. Her features were lean and bony, and her hair was cut in a stark bob that could scarcely be less complimentary. She seemed to glory in a coarse demeanor, which implied that if she could not be feminine and pretty, then she would be as absolutely *un*feminine and *un*pretty as possible. One Sunday supplement article in Dallas said:

Her lines and features are almost wholly masculine, a husky voice, a direct manner of speech that often drops into the sporting argot and an almost complete absence of feminine frills heighten the impression of masculinity. She follows no particular plan with her clothes and in this connection, a male reporter once got all tangled up trying to ask her a question. "Uh, Miss Didrikson, do you select – uh –your private – uh apparel with any special care? I mean do you – er – find that binding garments – er – what I mean is . . ." The poor man was blushing and stuttering in evident embarrassment. "Are you trying to ask me," said Babe in her straight-to-the-point fashion, "if I wear girdles, brassieres and the rest of that junk?" "Y-y-y-es," spluttered the reporter in sudden relief. "The answer is no," she snapped. "What do you think I am, a sissy?"

Babe was also quoted in that article saying, "I know I'm not pretty, but I do try to be graceful." Perhaps there was a note of wistfulness there that she would never be a "glamour girl," a term that was just catching on then. But if Babe felt cheated of glamour, her reaction was never passive or ladylike; there was no sniffling into scented hankies.

As the season of 1931–32 was to begin, many of Babe's teammates found her swaggering, me-first attitude insufferable. A woman who played with the Golden Cyclones, Mrs. Reagan Glenn of Seagoville,

Texas, recalled in an interview: "I admit I admired Babe because of all the things she could do. But some of the other gals really resented her. She was this masculine person, but she had it in her to be a champion, the ability was there all right, honey. She had great strength. She was born to run, to jump. She was built up by this man McCombs. He was a sharp-faced man and he worked us hard. People always ask me if Babe was the best player on the Cyclones and I say, 'Naw.' See, we had some wonderful guards. Honey, as far as basketball went, Babe was good, she was fast, she could hit the basket. But honey, she was *not* the best player. She got all the publicity in basketball, that's true. Why? Well she was the center forward and this position made her show up. She was masculine and she was an individual – she was out for Babe, honey, just Babe. We played as a team, we played as one. But I don't know how her mind run. She was not a team player, definitely not. Babe she was out for fame. There were lots of players on the Cyclones more popular than Babe was. But she got to be famous. And that's what she wanted."

The Golden Cyclones apparently made no secret of their distaste for Babe. On October 5, 1931, she wrote:

Dearest Tiny – Hello old top how is Beaumont coming – it should be okey eh! Heck I'm tired of this old Burg. Wish I could get out of it as soon as possible. Saw an advertisment in the Billboard wanting "Girl Athletes" and that they would give good salary at this place in Ohio. heck I could get a lot of good places if Colonel McCombs wouldn't try and make me professional. He can't though because I haven't done anything to make me one.

Heck, "Tiny" if I get me another letter from Wichita, Kans. I'm Gonna take it. Because I would like it better up there. These girls here are just like they were in Beaumont High School. Jealous and more so because they are all here and trying to beat me. But they can't do it.

Have you talked to Mr. Yount or Mr. Lee [two millionaires whose fortunes grew from the gushers of Spindletop II] I bet the boys would like to back me they should have lots of dough or some club or something of that kind. What you say "Tiny" lets get into some action and try and get me out of this place. And then maybe someday I'll come back then and whip the socks off the whole bunch. I remain, yours very truly, Babe Didrikson.

As the winter wore on, Babe's days grew darker. On New Year's Day of 1932 – the year that would bring her the most triumphant moments of her life – she wrote a sad, peevish letter:

Dearest Tiny: Well, Heck it seems as though I'm gonna have to go somewhere else. They think that I'm just putting them on up here and know I won't go. But I'm gonna show 'em I could get at least 50 more dollars out of 'em if I had a way to do it. I've got to make something of my athletic ability now or never – I'm not gonna be good always you know. I don't care whether I play basketball anymore or not. I'm sitting on the bench most of the game now because I won't try to play ball – I play about a half or more and won't make a shot. I miss everyone of them cause I don't want to play with them for nothing. I'm not gonna play at all – I might as well go on out for track and that will be all I'm gonna do cause I'm tired of working & giving them all this advertisement for nothing – $90.00 a month it's terrible – I've told them I was gonna leave but they don't seem to think I know what I'm talking about – but maybe they will after the first of Feb.

How's Mrs. Francis. Tell her thanks for the Christmas card and I appreciate yours too. How about a bunch of those write ups you have their of me. I am ready for them. I've finished all my others. Well, Tiny if you have time write me and tell me what you want me to do. Babe.

Babe's pay was actually fairly substantial. At $1,080 a year, she was getting more than double what some steelworkers got in 1932

($422.87), almost as much as an average schoolteacher ($1,227) and five times more than many farmhands ($220). Her salary of $90 a month could be stretched quite nicely: milk was a dime a quart, sirloin steak 29 cents a pound, a pair of leather women's shoes could be gotten for $1.79 and a wool dress for $1.95. Still, 1932 was the bleakest year of the Depression and Babe could scarcely ignore the desperate state of life around her. The roads were full of drifting hobos, some of them young women who became ten-cent prostitutes to survive. President Hoover insisted that everything was rosy, but his very name had become a symbol of poverty and dejection: the cardboard shantytowns that grew on the edge of many major cities were called "Hoovervilles"; stringy jackrabbits that hungry farmers were often forced to eat were called "Hoover hogs"; empty pockets turned inside out were "Hoover flags." The most popular song of the year was "Brother, Can You Spare a Dime?"

The depressed state of the nation was not Babe's only economic problem. She was also under personal siege from home to send all the money she could manage. Ruth Scurlock recalled, "Babe's family was really on their uppers all of the time. They always had their hands out to her – even in those years in Dallas when she was still practically a child making a pittance pay. She was under a lot of pressure all the time. She never had as much money as they thought she did, but they wanted her to give, give, give."

Despite these pressures and her own short-lived refusal to play well for Colonel McCombs and the Golden Cyclones, Babe ultimately performed brilliantly during the 1932 basketball season. Her team was runner-up in the national championship for the second time and she was once again an All American.

It is true that Colonel McCombs and Employers Casualty Company had exploited her talents to gain publicity, and their reputations were nicely gilded in reflection of Babe's (and the team's) magnificent performances. It is true, too, that the Colonel and the company probably should have paid her more money than they did, given her immense value to them. Yet, in fact, they had repaid her contribution to them many, many times over. For Babe Didrikson could not have become the superlative athlete she did without the equipment, the coaching, the encouragement, the financial backing, the competitive arena that McCombs and Employers Casualty offered her during those formative two and half years. There was never any question that McCombs himself knew precisely the kind of genius he was dealing with – from the start. He once told a reporter: "I have been involved with athletes of all kinds since the year 1904, but never before in my life have I seen a man or a woman to compare with Babe Didrikson for natural ability. In grasping, understanding and executing the most technical details of what she is taught, she has no equal. Her only fault, as I have found it, is that she unconsciously and unknowingly overtrains. Also Babe's juvenility and nervous energy ofttimes work to her disadvantage. She has a tendency to brood over coming events and even though she is not training on the field, her thoughts and tenseness generate her whole being into a seething fervor and unless continually cautioned she loses the spark that has carried her like a sweeping meteor to the very pinnacle of success."

Despite such hyperbole, the Colonel was a modest, low-keyed man who seemed to consider himself more an educator than a fire-and-brimstone leader. He was no Svengali and took little personal credit for Babe's success. He said, "Any coach who understands the fundamentals of what he is teaching and is able to gain the confidence and admiration of his pupil could have done just as much as I have. It was merely a case of smoothing out the surface. The glitter and brilliance was underneath."

Despite the Colonel's smooth recitals in Babe's behalf, the friction between them continued into the Olympic summer. Barely a month before her one-woman-team triumphs at the 1932 national women's track and field meet at Evanston, Babe quit her job, storming out in a tantrum because the Colonel had refused to reward her with an extra week's vacation for her fine performances. The Colonel protested that the company had already arranged to pay all of her expenses over a six-week period that included the national meet and the Olympics in Los Angeles. A day or two after she stalked out, Babe returned. The Associated Press reported: "Mildred changed her mind, came back to Dallas and said she was sorry. She cried over the telephone. She appeared at her office chastened and demure, to apply for reinstatement. Colonel M. J. McCombs said everything was all right. He expects much of the girl at the Los Angeles games."

She had become a prima donna: petulant, unreasonable. If the years with Employers Casualty had sharpened her athletic skills, they had also put some jagged edges on her personality. The metamorphosis can be seen clearly enough in her letters to Tiny, but the change in Babe was also apparent to those who competed against her. Evelyne Hall was a hurdler of Olympic caliber who raced against Babe a number of times. In 1975, Mrs. Hall was sixty-six, short and buxom, a graying, wholesome-looking matron, married for more than forty years to a retired paleontologist; they lived in Pasadena in a home decorated with many crocheted doilies and knickknacks. Mrs. Hall had begun track competition in 1926, with the 80-yard high-hurdles as her specialty. She first met Babe at the 1930 national women's meet, saw her again at the 1931 competition in Jersey City, then again at Evanston in 1932.

Mrs. Hall was in a unique position to observe the transformations that occurred from one year to the next during that essential formative period with Employers Casualty. She recalled: "At the A.A.U. meet in nineteen thirty, Babe was wearing a bright yellow suit with Employers Casualty Insurance written on it, she was sprawled on the ground and her teammates were around her. They were very proud and they kept saying what a great ball player she was. I liked her, too. At this time, she was a modest, likeable girl. She was lanky and boyish-looking with very short hair, but that was the style then. After the meet she wrote me a couple of letters, telling me about her family. She even sent me a couple of snapshots of them. I didn't compete against her in the nineteen thirty meet, she was not doing the hurdles then.

"The next time I saw Babe was in Jersey City, in nineteen thirty-one. It was a full house and the spectators got out of hand. They poured out of the stands onto the field and the mounted police had to be called to restore order, the horses ruined the track, a discus thrower hit a spectator with a discus. It was just bedlam. This was the first time Babe was in the hurdles with me. In our heat, she took three steps between hurdles and I took four; she was about four inches taller than I was. When she took three steps, I did too. My timing went all off and I hit a hurdle. We finished one, two. My foot swelled so that it broke the shoelaces on my track shoe. At this point, Babe was pretty cocky. Everybody was doing things for her. If she wanted a drink of water, someone got it for her. She seemed to have managers; her teammates waited on her. She didn't snub me, but she was not nearly as friendly to me as the year before. Our team had driven to New Jersey from Chicago and we did not have coaches or managers with us. We didn't have any money. We were poor. We each had a pair of track shoes, but the points were worn down to nothing. I remember Babe had the longest spikes of anyone, and they were very sharp. I remember I didn't have the money to get mine sharpened. When I had first met Babe in Dallas I liked to hear her talk in that slow Southern drawl. By nineteen thirty-one I think that drawl was gone. They had started to promote her.

"In nineteen thirty-two the national A.A.U. meet and the Olympic tryouts were in Evanston and we suddenly heard that they were going to let Babe compete in as many events as she wanted. Oh, we were mad because we had always been limited to three events. Well, Babe kept bragging that she was going to win them all. She made us so mad. When Babe won two events, we girls were even more annoyed that she was allowed to enter six others. She was eliminating other girls from a chance for an Olympic berth. She was getting special treatment from the officials, too. They'd hold up an event to wait for her and let her rest from the last one. She had such advantages, and she acted as if the world owed it all to her. I didn't like Babe anymore. The childish girl I met in Dallas in nineteen thirty was gone. She had been so nice then."

The 1932 A.A.U. meet was the vehicle for Babe's ascension to immortality at an early age. For the trip, she bought a frilly pink hat, her first. This was insisted upon by the official chaperone of the Golden Cyclones, Mrs. Henry Wood, who traveled to Chicago with Babe. The two women checked into a Chicago hotel the day before the meet. That night Babe developed an excruciating pain in her stomach. Her diaphragm began palpitating. Around dawn, she and Mrs. Wood called the hotel doctor. Casually enough, he diagnosed the problem as being the result of "nerves" and as the sky turned light, Babe finally fell asleep. Both she and Mrs. Wood overslept and they had to make a frantic ride to Dyche Stadium in Evanston in a taxi. Babe changed into her track togs beneath a blanket in the back seat, afraid she wouldn't have time at the stadium.

Despite all this tension and all the pressure, she recalled in her autobiography: "It was one those days in an athlete's life when you know you're just right. You feel you could fly. You're like a feather floating in the air."

There was bitter resentment among the other women that she was allowed to enter so many events, and her arrogance did not help her popularity. But Babe seemed to have mystical powers that day. Of the eight events she entered, the only one she failed to place in was the 100-yard dash. She had rarely performed in the shot put or the discus. On this exalted day she placed fourth in the discus to gain one point, then astonished everyone by winning the shot put with a toss of 39 feet, 6¼ inches. Next she won the baseball throw, with a throw of 272 feet, 2 inches, breaking her own record. She won the broad jump with a leap of 17 feet, 6 inches. She threw the javelin 139 feet, 3 inches, which beat her own world record. She then ran her first heat in the 80-meter hurdles in 11.9 seconds, another world mark.

In the finals of the hurdles, with Evelyne Hall as her primary rival, Babe's mystical powers also included a large dose of good luck. Mrs. Hall recalled: "They had two judges for each place in the hurdle race – two calling first place, two second, two third, et cetera. When the race was over the judges huddled at the finish line and we crowded around. They went through the finishers and suddenly one of them asked, 'Where's Didrikson?' I don't know what happened, if they missed her or what. But all of a sudden they took first place away from me and gave me second. They put Babe in first. I was too shy and modest to complain, but I think since she was expected by the judges to be the star, it was a foregone conclusion that she won it. There was never a film of the race. I don't know where she really finished."

After the hurdles, Babe broke one more world record – in the high jump. She and Jean Shiley of Temple University tied at 5 feet, 3³⁄₁₆ inches.

It was an unforgettable display. She had won six gold medals and broken four world records in the space of three hours in a single afternoon. The United Press reporter George Kirsey sent a dispatch in which he described it as "the most amazing series of performances ever accomplished by any individual, male or female, in track and field history." And, as the women selected for the Olympic team prepared to leave Chicago for Los Angeles, the Associated Press reported: "Miss Mildred Didrikson of Dallas, Tex., who prefers to be called 'Babe', will lead the American women's Olympic track and field team. Such assistance as she may need against the foreign invasion will be provided by fifteen other young ladies."

Of course, the "other young ladies" did not take warmly to Babe's being anointed by the press as their "leader." Most of them did not like her and the train ride to the West Coast eventually became a rather acrimonious affair. Nevertheless, it was a heady, exciting time for all of them.

The team traveled in a private railroad car with an enormous red, white and blue banner on the side that said U.S. OLYMPIC TEAM. When the train thundered across the plains of Illinois and Kansas toward Denver, dozens of people turned out in the hamlets and towns of the Midwest to wave at these heroines. The young Olympians were mostly greenhorns, unsophisticated homegrown girls who rarely traveled far and had vivid expectations about what they would see on this fantastic journey across the country. Even Babe, who had been on many trips with the Golden Cyclones, was full of wonderful hick-town notions. "I was looking forward to seeing 'The Mile High City' of Denver," she said. "It sounds silly now, but I expected to see a city that was built a mile up in the air."

Evelyne Hall recalled the trip: "We used to spend the days walking through the cars to the observation decks at the rear. We felt like millionaires. It was a dream. When we got to Denver we took a trip out to Pike's Peak. This was the first time I had ever been west of the Mississippi. I took one look at those mountains and I was on cloud nine. Once we stopped – I think it was in Albuquerque – and we all just had to get out of the train. We just had to step foot in another state.

"Babe was very full of herself and on the train she was always pulling pranks. She delighted in yanking the pillow out from under your head when you were asleep. She and Gloria Russell, a javelin competitor, also used to throw pillows at the girls. They especially liked to throw them at girls who wouldn't retaliate. The pillows would get caught on the hooks attached to the berths; they'd split open and we had feathers all over the car.

"When we all got out in Albuquerque, Babe got out too, and she spotted a Western Union bicycle on the platform. She jumped on it and started beating her chest and screaming at the top of her lungs: 'Did you ever hear of Babe Didrikson? If you haven't you will! You w-i-i-i-l-l-l-l!' It was so embarrassing. She also used to take ice from the water cooler and drop it down our backs."

As the trip went on, the hostility toward Babe increased. Jean Shiley Newhouse, the high jumper and team captain, a tall, angular woman with a husky voice, still had bitter memories of Babe when she was interviewed in 1975. She said: "I had never even noticed her before we competed in Evanston; that was the first time she was in the high jump in the nationals. In the beginning I felt sorry for her because the others were downgrading her so badly. I had to room with her in Denver because no one else would. Then as time went on I realized she certainly did have a big mouth. She would horn in every two minutes. If someone said they rode a kayak down from Alaska in three days, Babe would have done it better. She had no social graces whatsoever. She constantly wanted to be on center stage. In Colorado, a radio interviewer was trying to talk to each member of the team, separately. He talked to Babe and finished, but then she kept horning in on the other interviews. When the reporter ignored her, Babe stood there and played her harmonica to call attention to herself; the noise drowned out the other girls' answers, of course.

"I have often wondered *why* she was so obnoxious. Maybe she never got the attention she needed as a child, or maybe she was trying to psych us out — although that was not a term anyone had ever heard of then. It was impossible to get to know her because she was always chattering, talking, bragging. There was never a chance for a dialogue. She ran around with her medals from Evanston, saying, 'I'm the greatest, no one's better than me, Babe Didrikson.' Today, I don't think her behavior would seem so outrageous. People are used to flamboyant athletes. In those days, athletes were supposed to be full of humility and modesty. Now we are used to people like Muhammad Ali and Jimmy Connors and Ilie Nastase.

"On the trip out, Babe's name came up to be elected captain of the team. I had been nominated and so had Lillian Copeland, our shot putter. Lillian told me privately that she was going to withdraw her name from the election. She said that if she didn't Babe might win in a three-way split of the votes and that we just could not have that. She withdrew and I won. If Babe had won, the team would have been simply torn apart."

Throughout the games, Babe Didrikson was to remain a thorn to women of the American team and they came to detest her. As for the rest of the people in the world, she suddenly burst into bloom as a singularly fine rose and they came to adore her.

Chapter 6

It was in Los Angeles during the 1932 Olympics that the legend of Babe Didrikson was sculpted, gilded and boosted to its pedestal for all time. She was practically canonized. From today's cool vantage point it may seem overwrought or overblown, but it was logical and in tune with the moment in which she performed. The environment of 1932 lent itself to the flowering of sports legends.

During the first half of the twentieth century, sport had played a part in American life that was almost as important as religion. Sport was not only America's diversion, it was also its illusion, its symbol of hope. Unlike the contemporary conflicts of politics, business, and war, and unlike the eternal conflict of good versus evil, the conflicts of sport were visible, tangible, comprehensible, manageable. They had a concrete beginning, a foreseeable end, an unmistakable result. It was the conventional wisdom of the day to see sport as a "microcosm of life," as an accurate reflection of what could happen if Americans applied their highest ideals, their purest motives, to some tangible pursuit. This childlike view has been replaced in recent years by deep cynicism as many of the best American athletes have proved to be merely acquisitive wealthy businessmen while their games have, in large part, become vehicles for selling products on television. Yet in the days of the Depression, sports and its heroes offered inspiration as well as escape.

The pageantry of sports, the constant celebration of selfless sacrifice and high moral purpose, the obvious rewards for stick-to-itiveness and valor and virtue and teamwork, the praise for hard work and fair play – these simplistic things offered a vision of hope to people mired in the No-Exit despair of the Depression. In sports, they could see mere mortals winning against heavy odds, against hardship, pain, bad luck. Even though the microcosm sports offered was perfectly artificial and scarcely related to reality at all, such visible manifestations of man emerging victorious over his destiny offered at least the possibility that real life, too, could be conquered.

This was a tenuous connection at best, but perhaps the Depression escapism of sports was really not any less hopeful than that offered by formal religions of the day. At any rate, Babe Didrikson's star rose because of it.

Another essential factor in her elevation to legend had deeper roots in history. For many, many years the population of the world – and of the United States particularly – had been moving away from the role of participants in sports to that of spectators. This rise – and ultimate reign – of the spectator is the greatest basic change in sports to occur in hundreds of years.

Mankind has had a long love affair with games and sports but spectatorship has had an inconsistent history. The ancient Olympic Games began in 776 B.C. as a provincial event on the order of a country fair. Eventually the Games attracted forty thousand spectators to Olympia. Philosophers (the sports writers of the day) wrote of the fierce heat, cramped space, the noises and worst of all the lack of drinking water. The multitudes in ancient Greece sat on hillsides to watch the spectacle and they spent the night in a city of tents erected nearby. Because of this massive spectator interest, the athletes of Greece became a pampered class of swaggering narcissists who did little but build their bodies and massage their egos from one year to the next. They were immortalized in marble; Pindar wrote odes to them; the public adored them. But eventually their glorification cooled. The philosopher Xenophanes complained that the culture of Greece had reached a point where people praised a wrestler's strength over a philosopher's wisdom, and Aristotle criticized the life of athletic specialization. The Greek Olympics lasted for 1,168 years. Until our own twentieth-century Olympics, only ancient Rome exceeded Greece for overall magnitude of spectatorship in sports. The Circus Maximus held three hundred and fifty thousand people when filled; this was the largest crowd ever to view any single event in the history of the world – until television elevated spectating to a life-style. The Romans enjoyed more violence than anything offered on television today; the fan was delighted by lions, tigers, elephants and crocodiles devouring each other – or doing the same to defenseless criminals, prisoners of war or Christians. At the gala opening of the Colosseum, nine thousand animals were butchered while thousands of spectators cheered. Rome wallowed in spectator blood-lust for several centuries, but once the empire fell the world seemed sated with sporting extravaganzas. Throughout the Dark Ages and well into the nineteenth century people did most of their spectating at church or at public hangings or executions. (Some thirty thousand turned out to watch Marie Antoinette be guillotined.) There were country fairs and jousting tournaments, but lavish sporting events specifically designed for the spectators did not surface again until the French aristocrat Baron Pierre de Coubertin launched the modern Olympic Games in Athens in 1896. By then the industrial revolution had left its mark on mankind. The city had become the center of society; people crowded together to be near the factories. There was at long last leisure time. At first these leisure hours were spent in personal participation in games, but soon this palled for many millions. Rather than play games, many chose to spend their leisure time sitting, watching their favorite team play, enjoying vicariously the excellence of others.

Around the year Babe was born, 1911, America's first big stadiums were going up. In 1914 Yale built the Bowl, the first really modern stadium, with eighteen miles of seats. College football was *the* American spectator sport early in the twentieth century. The stadiums for baseball were not really large until 1923, when Yankee Stadium, the House that Ruth built, was dedicated. It could seat sixty-five thousand. By the 1920s sports in America had become more an entertainment medium than a form of personal physical exercise. As such it stood halfway between the theater, with its stars, and war, with its heroes. It was artificial in that it was staged and ballyhooed as if it were drama, yet it was real in that its results, its climaxes, its crises contained a real element of risk, of violence – and thus a possibility for real heroics.

At the same time the country was building its first gargantuan stadiums – not unlike cathedrals of sport – the phenomenon of mass communications was making itself felt. In the early 1920s, there was no single road that connected the nation from coast to coast, but there was the telegraph and there was radio and there were newspapers. The impact of radio would reach its peak in the later 1930s and 1940s, but in the era that came to be called The Golden Age of Sport (Babe appeared at the end) it was the newspaper that brought The Word to the world. Because of the general insistence that everyone receive at least an eighth-grade education, the number of Americans able to read was enormously large compared to any other civilization in the history of the world. Everyone read the paper; everyone believed its reports to be gospel.

These were rich and exciting days for newspapermen. They were among the most influential people in the country. They were not above exploiting their readers, however.

This era spawned the tabloids, a sensational breed of newspaper that was first born with the New York *Daily News*. The *News* appeared in 1919 and ten years later it had a million readers, the largest circulation in the country. Dozens of imitators sprang up in the 1920s. They all dispensed the same brand of lip-smacking scandal and hyped-up stories of murder-most-foul. They thrived on the Leopold-Loeb murder, the axe murders of Winnie Ruth Judd, the Lindbergh kidnapping. They doted on the fate of Floyd Collins, a luckless Kentuckian who was trapped in an underground honeycomb near Mammoth Cave for eighteen days in 1925 while he slowly died of exposure. The tabloids gave their readers a daily freak show of the afflicted, the dead, the criminal, the insane.

These were crazy days in the country: fads abounded, and journalists were eager to scoop each other by covering every scrap of foolishness. Long-distance dancing, long-distance walking ("Bunion Derbies"), rocking-chair derbies made news. There were page-one stories about the world's champion pea-eater, about yo-yo tricks, about a man in Minnesota who claimed a world record after he bobbed up and down in the water 1,843 times. Crossword puzzles were a craze and papers covered college teams locked in mortal conflict at crossword puzzle tournaments. Flagpole sitting captured headlines and the celebrated "Shipwreck" Kelley made the front page when he married a shop girl who was lifted up his flagpole for an introduction. (Six years later the papers covered their divorce with equal intensity and quoted the

A dropout at eighteen, Babe went to Dallas to seek her fortune as a semiprofessional athlete for the Employers Casualty Company. Soon she was the star and wrote home, "I'm going to enter every kind of meet and get full of medals. You know like ants."

At the 1932 Olympics, Babe lost the gold medal in the high jump when the judges ruled she dived illegally (above). In the 80-meter hurdles (opposite) Evelyne Hall got off to a fast start, but Babe caught her at the tape to win a disputed goal.

In starstruck Los Angeles, Babe came to be known as "Whatta-Gal" after winning gold medals in the javelin and hurdles. Above, she poses on the victory stand with arch rival Evelyne Hall (left).

Babe and other Olympic heroines hobnobbed with celebrities of press and show biz in Los Angeles. Above, from left: swimmer Helene Madison, sportswriting "Dean" Grantland Rice, Babe, Will Rogers, diver Georgia Coleman, Braven Dyer of the Los Angeles Times. Her jubilant post-Olympic reception at the Dallas airport (right) was attended by local kingfish who lauded her as "the Jim Thorpe of women athletes."

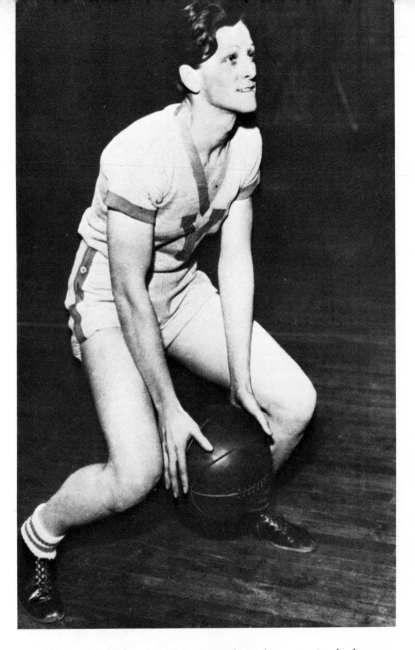

After the Games, she took to the road as a barnstorming basketball player and later as a pitcher for the House of David baseball team.

Babe won her first golf tournament in Texas at twenty-three. Her game was strong, but she was snubbed by many in the country-club set because of her origins in Beaumont's South End. Off the course, she was always willing to spend hours with children, teaching them how to swing a club or pitch a baseball.

former Mrs. Kelley as saying, "What's the use of having a husband unless he comes home nights?") Mah-Jongg, contract bridge, and marathon dancing received lots of coverage.

Perhaps the United Press reached the highest point of zaniness for the whole decade when it filed a dispatch from Warsaw, Indiana, which informed the nation, coast to coast and border to border: "Clarence Tillman, 17, a local high school student, put 40 sticks of chewing gum in his mouth at one time, sang, 'Home Sweet Home' and between verses of the song drank a gallon of buttermilk."

Babe Didrikson, like the heroes, villains and sensation-seekers, was also a product of journalism and journalists. It is true that, compared to the steamy tabloids, most papers in the country were relatively respectable and responsible in their news coverage. They did their share and more to propagate all manner of harmless loony doings, but when straight news was involved, editors and reporters usually wrapped themselves in the pallid robes of "objectivity" and told what happened without particular embroidery. Except on the sports page. Nowhere in America was there a sport page that simply told what happened; all dealt in the purplest hyperbole and glorification of athletes. Newspapers printed a daily paean to this superrace of sportsmen, a kind of endless bedtime story rampant with reports of living legends with such delightful names as Galloping Ghost, Sultan of Swat, Manassa Mauler. The dispensing of on-the-spot immortality was common, and most sportswriters engaged in the constant building and gilding of supermyths.

The leading ladler of such syrup was Grantland Rice. He was best known for his verse and though it rarely rose more than a razor thin cut above the rhyming roadside signs of Burma Shave, it was memorized by youngsters, declaimed by coaches and carved in stone above countless high school gymnasium doors. His best-known verse was: *"When the One Great Scorer comes to write against your name he marks – not that you won or lost – but how you played the game."* It was also Granny Rice who composed the single best-known lead paragraph in sportswriting history. After Knute Rockne's 1924 Notre Dame backfield defeated powerful Army, he wrote: "Outlined against a blue-grey October sky, the Four Horsemen rode again. In dramatic lore they are known as Famine, Pestilence, Destruction and Death. These are only aliases. Their real names are Stuhldreher, Miller, Crowley and Layden."

Such magnification of mere men, mere college boys playing a game, was de rigueur. Even the toughest writers showed no cynicism, only prostrate worship, when confronted by a great athlete. For instance Damon Runyon wrote: "What a football player – this man Red Grange. He is melody and symphony. He is a crashing sound. He is brute force." O. B. Keeler wrote of Bobby Jones's mastery of golf: "Looking back over Bobby's matches, you may see crisis after crisis where the least slip in nerve or skill or plain fortune would have spelled blue ruin to Bobby's dearest ambition. Yet at every crisis he stood up to the shot with something which I can define only as inevitability and performed what was needed with all the certainty of a natural phenomenon." Even the horses of the time were not mere mortal nags: Man o' War was described as "the horse of eternity."

It was all a mixture of Barnum colossalism and American boosterism, Greek mythology and Holy-Roller evangelism.

Everyone took the sportsman to be a substantial cut above the common man. As a Methodist minister once said, "If St. Paul were living today, he would know Babe Ruth's batting average and what yardage Red Grange made."

Nothing before or since – certainly not the cool, cool waves of television – has created such a hot romance between sports stars and the public as the printed word did during the rising heyday of Babe Didrikson.

All told, her timing could not have been better. This was an era of innocence, goofiness and uncontained adoration of celebrities. That the nation was wallowing in the pits of the Depression worked to give her leap to stardom extra impetus. What better medicine for a weary and discouraged nation than a huge dose of the Olympic panoply – brass bands blaring, marching ranks of tanned and healthy athletes, gaudy flags snapping in the California sunshine? This was the escapism of sport in quantum size.

Chapter
7

The Tenth Olympiad extended from July 30 to August 14, 1932 and drew 1,980 athletes from thirty-seven countries. By contrast, the 1936 Olympics held in Berlin under the aegis of Hitler's Nazi impressarios attracted more than 4,000 participants. Nevertheless, the Los Angeles Games were really quite colossal, the first of the lavish Olympic spectaculars that have come to be expected each four years. These were the first Olympics to turn a profit: more than one million dollars. And the setting was impressive. The Coliseum had been especially enlarged and renovated; it was ballyhooed as having "thirty miles of seats."

Los Angeles had been campaigning for twelve years to get the Games and, Depression or not, the city was not to be denied. The chairman of the local organizing committee was a former cowboy named Zack Farmer. He said, "Hell, Chicago tried to steal the Games from us as late as two years before they started. They told the International Olympic Committee we were going to flop out here, that the climate was too hot. Westbrook Pegler, he was with the Chicago Tribune Syndicate, and he was sent by Colonel McCormick to blow us out of the water. Of course, I admit we were a noisy, blatant damn town that annoyed everybody in the country, I'll admit that."

The "City of Angeles" was already a mecca of seedy hedonism where people gorged themselves on tales of overnight fame and instant immortality. Although the first freeway had yet to be built, the familiar stucco sprawl that is L.A. today was already moving across vast acres. The population of Los Angeles in 1932 was 1,300,000: there were almost no natives; most Angelenos' roots had been pulled up somewhere else. In Los Angeles there were no traditions, no weight of history to hold things down. Everything was temporal, ticky-tacky architecture bathed in sunshine.

The city doted on movie stars, their assignations, their opinions, their appetites. Hollywood had a delicious reputation for glamorous sin, but the movie colony was not quite so morally unbuttoned as many believed. The most suggestive movie line of 1932 occured in *Night After Night,* starring George Raft and Mae West, when a friend remarked, "Goodness, what beautiful diamonds!" and Mae cooed, "Goodness has nothing to do with it, dearie." The top box-office stars of the year were Marie Dressler, Janet Gaynor, Charles Farrell, Greta Garbo and Joan Crawford. Fred Astaire had not even been to Hollywood yet; Shirley Temple was still appearing in one-reelers called *Baby Burlesks.*

Had the Games of 1932 been held in Antwerp or Amsterdam or even Paris – anywhere that was a normal working, earthbound city – it is questionable whether Babe Didrikson would have caused the sensation she did. But Los Angeles, with its Hollywood backdrop, was perfect; it offered a marvelous Olympic milieu, a dazzling mixture of glamorous movie stars and exotic athletes. The Flying Finn, Paavo Nurmi, who had won seven gold medals in three previous Olympics, arrived in L.A. and was promptly outlawed from the Games for professionalism. He stayed on, glowering, in hopes that the ruling might be reversed but it was not. Duke Kahanamoku, the fabulous

Hawaiian swimmer who had won medals as far back as 1912 and again in 1920 and 1924, was back at the age of forty-two to compete on the American water polo team. Japan's Takeichi Nishi, a magnificent horseman and army officer, was a dashing figure and a Hollywood favorite. He was lionized by Mary Pickford and Douglas Fairbanks; Will Rogers was his friend. Nishi was only a lieutenant in the Japanese cavalry but he had been born a baron; Douglas Fairbanks said, "One Baron Nishi is worth ten diplomats."

The Japanese were endlessly fascinating to journalists and movie stars alike, a genuine novelty. Japanese men swimmers ("merry little brown fellows") won eleven of the twelve gold medals and everyone was genuinely baffled. One sportswriter explained their success with succinct expertise: "Having shorter legs than most swimmers, the Japanese need not put their head down so far for balance as do the longer-limbed Americans. This enables them to swim higher in the water which promotes far more speed." The Japanese women did not win any races at all but one reporter gushed: "They have shown such admirable sportsmanship that they have won the hearts of thousands of spectators. And now comes their reward. Each is going to have her shiny, black, straight hair permanently waved by a Southern California beauty expert."

The Los Angeles papers covered the Olympics in the manner in which they had been accustomed to covering Hollywood. They revealed that Olympic "starlets" were doing their own laundry in their rooms at the Chapman Park Hotel, scrubbing hotel soap bars "to slivers in no time flat." One feature writer compared the regimen of Olympic athletes to that of hopeful budding starlets: "When a Hollywood girl goes in training for a big 'meet' – an important starring role in a love drammer for Peerless Passion Pictures, Inc. – she concentrates heavily on lamb chops and pineapple or green salads with sour cream dressing. She wants to get thin. An Olympic athlete is different. They want not to be thin, not to be fat, but to be healthy."

Olympic girls were constantly being questioned about their "beauty diets." When Babe was asked about her beauty diet, she replied: "I eat anything I want – except greasy foods and gravy. I pass the gravy. That's just hot grease anyway, with some flour and water in it."

The women's Olympic teams were put up at the Chapman Park Hotel, a rather ordinary stucco apartment building. There was a flag-draped communal dining room for two hundred, a lobby replete with potted palms and an outdoor garden. During the Games, there were nightly entertainments at the Chapman featuring the songs and dances of different countries. American night, according to one reporter, included "Indians and war dances, log cabins, wild west stunts with such music as 'Yankee Doodle', 'Dixie' and negro spirituals." Try as they might to liven it up, the women's quarters were distinctly second-rate compared to the men's. The men lived in the Olympic Village, the first ever built. Though it was controversial at first, it became a great hit.

Zack Farmer recalled: "Foreigners were afraid of the idea. They squawked that they had training secrets and didn't want to live close together. They also said, 'By God, we don't believe you can ever discipline the American public to leave that Village alone and give us privacy.' They said Americans are known as the most undisciplined goddamn people in the whole world. Oh, but we got privacy for those athletes, all right. We fenced it all in and put cowboys on riding the fences. Those Europeans used to love to watch the cowboys lassoing any S.O.B. who tried to climb over the fence. That Village was the marvel of the Games. They wrote books about it in Europe afterwards. We damn near had to drive the athletes out to get them to go home after the Games. It was the most grand and pathetic thing you ever saw. Those big hulks practically cried when they had to leave. They *loved* it."

Everyone loved it. Damon Runyon visited the community of portable bunglows and gushed, "It is a glorious feast to the eye with the California sun sparkling on the flowers and on the wee pink and white houses." He also reported that "Naked young men are sprawled out here and there on the turf, all of them tanned the color of an old saddle. It is difficult to distinguish the Americans from the Argentines or the Japanese or the Filipinos. The California sun has painted them all alike." The village was for men only but two days after Runyon described this provocative scene a daring woman named Rosalind Brunswick slipped past Zack Farmer's mounted cowboys, climbed the ten-foot barbed-wire fence and strolled through the village asking for autographs. Inevitably, she was soon captured by a posse of grim cowboys on horseback. While grinning members of the Italian team looked on, Rosalind clung fiercely to a horse's bridle, nearly causing the animal to flip over in a cloud of dust. But she was subdued at last and forced to climb back out of the Village over the fence at the same point she had entered. A crowd of five hundred applauded her spunk.

Movie stars – "luminaries" – were everywhere. Tom Mix, the Marx Brothers, Gary Cooper, Clark Gable, Buster Keaton, Spanky McFarland and the entire Our Gang (including the dog with the monocle painted around one eye).

As usual, the stars were invited to enlighten the masses with their opinions. Douglas Fairbanks toured the Village with a reporter at his elbow and he spoke of many things: "The Greeks had the right idea – develop mind, body and emotions together. Literature for the mind, sports for the body, the theater, music, sculpture, painting for the emotions. Know why the Germans have such good teams? Method. System. When I was in Europe, I saw great athletic fields all over

Germany. Everybody exercises. Everybody is healthy and strong. Did you know that every athletic club and group in Sweden was originally a literary society? I found that out at a dinner they gave me in Stockholm. Aren't those Italians full of life and spirit? Benito Mussolini is responsible for that. Italy is like one vast college campus. Every country needs a benevolent dictator. But a Mussolini comes along only once in a lifetime. He cleaned up Italy, and now it's about the most popular country in Europe as far as travellers are concerned. He recognizes the need and value of sports. I look for Italy to make a marvelous showing in every event. A people as enthusiastic and as colorful as the Italians are certain to do big things. Mussolini gave the team a fight talk just before it left. He calls them 'Romans' and reminds them of Rome's glory. They'll be out there fighting for the honor of Romulus and Remus, Julius Caesar, Marc Antony and those other greats. . . ."

Even in this Hollywood sea of dross and glamour Babe Didrikson stood out. She became "Whatta Gal" Didrikson, the Texas Tornado, The Terrific Tomboy. She was outrageous, boastful, ceaselessly sounding off for reporters and radio broadcasters. They adored her, glorified her brashness and quoted her endlessly: "I came out to beat everybody in sight and that's just what I'm going to do. Sure I can do anything."

Just before the Games began, the New York *Times* ran a long story under her byline:

What I want to do most of all in the Olympics is to win four firsts – something no girl has ever done. If they will let me enter the discus throw [they didn't], I think I can do it. I am interested in so many events that it seems impossible to do justice to all of them. Often I enter an event just to pick up a few extra points. I had not tried the shot-put for a long time before the Chicago tryouts, but entered just to get more points and I took first. Naturally athletics have not left me much time for household tasks for which a girl is supposed to have some liking, but I do not care about them. If necessary, however, I can sew and cook. One of my dresses won first place in a Texas State contest in 1930. Much of the credit for my performances should go to Colonel M. J. McCombs of Dallas, my coach, who always has kept up my confidence by such remarks as this: "You can win that event — now get out there and do it." So far I guess he has not been disappointed.

She told the Associated Press: "Yep, I'm going to win the high jump Sunday and set a world record. I don't know who my opponents are and, anyways, it wouldn't make any difference. I hope they are good." Once she walked up to Helene Madison, who held fifteen world swimming records and asked her what her time was in the 100-meter freestyle; when Miss Madison replied, Babe snorted, "Shucks, lady, I can beat that by three seconds just practicin'!"

Every grandiose Texas-twanging boast enlarged her character and inflated her legend. She had a folksy, common touch, not unlike Will Rogers. Hers was a gap-toothed country wit, ingenuous yet cutting, the kind of native wile that allowed the country boy to one-up the city slicker every time. It is impossible to know now whether Babe was consciously promoting this facade or whether it was the genuine product of childlike outbursts of confidence. But her behavior was a balm to millions of flat-broke Americans. They were convinced they had been victimized by sophisticated Wall Street sharks and Washington bureaucrats. Babe's crude boasts carried an echo of cracker-barrel retaliation against the Establishment. She would say: "Folks say that I go about winning these athletic games because I have the cooperation thing that has to do with eye, mind and muscle. That sure is a powerful lot of language to use about a girl from Texas, maybe they are right about it. All I know is that I can run and I can jump and I can toss things and when they fire a gun or tell me to get busy I just say to myself, 'Well, kid, here's where you've got to win another.' And I usually do."

This sort of thing produced admiring guffaws through all the Tobacco Roads and Hoovervilles of America. She was producing her own myth; it lay somewhere between *You Know Me Al,* Pecos Bill and the unsinkable Molly Brown.

Chapter
8

The Tenth Olympiad opened with Vice President Charles Curtis as the official American host. President Hoover did not deign – or did not dare – to appear. It was the first time the chief of a host nation had not been present at the opening ceremonies, but two days earlier Washington, D.C. had been engulfed in battle. Police and troops led by General Douglas MacArthur, the former president of the U.S. Olympic Committee, engaged World War I veterans who were demanding early payment of a bonus due them. A man was shot to death and two babies died of tear gas poisoning in the fighting but this did not dampen the Olympic pageantry in Los Angeles.

Hours before the opening ceremonies were to begin, the Coliseum was sold out; 105,000 people poured into the stadium. It was the greatest crowd ever to see an Olympics, the greatest assembly of spectators since the heyday of the Roman Colosseum. A huge, white-robed chorus sang "The Star-Spangled Banner." Then cloud after cloud of doves, symbols of peace, was released. Trumpets blared. The Olympic flame was lighted and when U.S. Navy Lieutenant George Calnan spoke the Olympic oath many of the assembled athletes standing by national rank on the field intoned the words under their breath. The muttering in a dozen languages produced an eerie sound in the hushed stadium that was spine chilling. Babe Didrikson was not all that impressed. "To tell you the truth," she recalled later, "I couldn't enjoy the ceremonies that much after we got out there. We all had to wear special dresses and stockings and white shoes that the Olympic Committee had issued us. I believe that was about the first time I'd ever worn a pair of stockings in my life; I was used to anklets and socks. As for the shoes they were really hurting my feet." Babe solved the shoe dilemma by standing barefoot during the two-hour ceremony.

It was a sweltering hot day but the crowd was caught up in the Olympic fervor. A writer for the Los Angeles *Times* reported:

Just for once being a world-famous motion picture star was of no consequence whatever. Even dear old Joe E. Brown, so used to being the subject of excited nudges, with that amazing mouth of his in training to open capaciously for the delectation of his worshipers, was to realize the strange preoccupation of the crowd on this occasion. As he and Mrs. Brown emerged through the tunnel there was that little self-conscious squaring of the shoulders to receive the usual applause with grace. But even the ushers' attention wouldn't quite concentrate – and the Browns reached their seats minus all personal commotion.

To most the day seemed somehow sacred. A Los Angeles *Times* writer complained that the only dignitaries in the Coliseum to shed their coats, collars and "tilt their hats on the back of their heads and puff like a lot of sweating horses" were members of the Los Angeles City Council; "to some of us this was as sacrilegious as shedding one's raiment in church," said the reporter. Another offensive occurrence was "the extraordinary bad taste of the airplane advertisers – the one really cheap commercial note in what was otherwise an almost holy occasion."

The next day the competition began and Babe immediately lived up to her legend. Like Muhammad Ali, her body was able to accomplish the fantastic feats that her boastful big mouth set for it. On her very first try with the javelin, she unleashed a throw of 143 feet, 4 inches that broke the world record by more than eleven feet. When the public address announcer boomed this amazing result, a tremendous bellow rose through the stadium. Babe trotted about, her hands clasped high over her head. No one came close to matching that throw – including Babe. Her second and third attempts were feeble and people wondered if she was simply rubbing it into the other competitors by only half-trying. Her first throw had been strange, too, a low flying trajectory that lacked the high arc of a classic javelin throw. Later Babe explained to reporters who wondered if she had developed a new technique: "No, I haven't got a new technique. My hand slipped when I picked up the pole. It slid along about six inches and then I got a good grip again. And then I threw it and it just went." Years later, Babe revealed that she had not warmed up properly before the event. "Nobody knew it, but I tore a cartilage in my right shoulder when my hand slipped making that first throw. On my last two turns, people thought I wasn't trying because the throws weren't much good. But they didn't need to be."

Next – two days later – came the 80-meter hurdles; her chief rival was Evelyne Hall. On the train to Los Angeles Babe had told Evelyne that it was simple to win because the officials were all "stupid." She said, "All you have to do to win if it's close is throw up your arm just before the finish and they think you're first." Babe and Evelyne won their heats in world record times. In the finals they were in lanes side by side. At the gun, Evelyne Hall sped ahead and led by a stride over the first hurdles. Babe kept coming, her form more powerful than graceful, her face grim and strained. She pulled even over the last two hurdles, held her stride and the women hit the finish line absolutely in tandem. Babe threw up her arm. Both were timed in 11.7 seconds, another world record. Evelyne had a welt on her neck from hitting the tape. Had she finally beaten Babe? The judges huddled in confusion, then declared their decision. Babe had won her second gold medal.

In the spring of 1975, forty-three years later, Evelyne Hall recalled those moments and her eyes brimmed with tears. "After we crossed the line, Babe yelled to me, 'Well, I won again.' I turned and saw some athletes in the crowd cheering me, holding up one finger to show me that I was first. I shook my head and held up two fingers to them. Later, I learned that at that very moment a couple of judges were looking at me. It's possible they made their judgment from this gesture of mine. I really don't know. Babe had had so *much* publicity, it was impossible to rule against her. The judges were foreign and to them it didn't matter that much, we were both Americans. I was heartbroken. I have always been taught right is right and I felt, and still feel, that I was every bit the champion. My foot was over first and I broke the tape first."

Evelyne Hall was unlucky that afternoon and Babe Didrikson was not. It is impossible to tell from official films who won; perhaps a dead heat should have been called. But Babe had such momentum going then that there was an air of inevitability about every victory she scored. With two gold medals in two events, it seemed more than possible that she might win a third also – something no woman had ever done in Olympic track and field.

Her last event was the high jump; Jean Shiley was the woman she had to beat. The other competitors did not figure to be very close. By this time the dissension between Babe and most other members of the

American team had become even more intense than during the train ride west. Evelyne Hall recalled, "We were all actually praying for Jean Shiley to win. We were very high-strung and we put a lot of pressure on Jean to beat this obnoxious girl."

On the day of the event, all competitors except Babe and Jean dropped out by the time the bar was raised to 5 feet, 5¼ inches. Both girls cleared that height and it was a new world's record. The judges raised the bar to 5 feet, 6¼ inches. On her first jump, Babe flew over the bar with more than an inch to spare. She fell triumphantly to the pit – and then one foot kicked a stanchion and knocked the bar from the pegs. The judges ruled she had missed. Jean also missed. Now the judges dropped the bar back to 5 feet, 5¼ inches for a runoff to see which of the competitors would get the gold medal. Jean made it. Babe made it. Another tie? No. This time, the judges ruled that Babe had "dived" over the bar, an illegal jump. Her head went over before the rest of her body. The rule no longer exists, but on this technicality the gold medal was given to Jean Shiley, the silver to Babe; both were eventually made co-holders of the world record.

Babe's friends in the press thought the decision was wrong, that Babe clearly deserved the gold medal. Frank G. Menke wrote angrily: "She twice shattered the world's record for the high jump and then was deprived of the high jump honors by two weird rulings by officials." Babe herself was confused and in an interview with Menke, she said: "For the first time since I've been in athletics I am a bit mixed up ... where I am all twisted is how did the judges come to make two rulings against me on two different jumps? The first time I went over clean and landed on the ground. I never wiggled the bar. But as I hit the ground, one of my legs popped out from under me and it kicked against a post and the jarring post caused the bar to fall. The way I look at it, from what I know of the rules, that was a clean jump and it should have been credited to me because the bar did not fall due to any blunder on my part when clearing it." About the ruling on her "dive" Babe said, "I jumped in all parts of the United States before some of the best judges in the country and they all approved that method and even the judges out there Sunday afternoon [at the Olympics] had nothing to say about it until I had twice cleanly cleared the bar."

Jean Shiley saw it differently. When she spoke of the event in the spring of 1975, there were no tears; her voice was chill and her face was stiff. She said: "Babe would never even have tied me if I'd done what the Canadian girl and the German girl [other jumpers that day] told me to do. They said I just had to tell the officials that her jumps were illegal. All of her jumps over five feet were dives. Even our coach – George Vreeland – sent me a note down from the stands and told me that Babe was fouling and that I should turn her in. Well, I couldn't do that. I knew she'd clobber me – with her mouth – if I caused her to lose by claiming a foul. When the officials ruled she had dived, Babe left the field very, very angry. The other girls on the team were delighted, like children at Christmas because I had beaten Babe. I was under terrible pressure, you know, because they had spent the last two days in my room saying, 'We couldn't beat her, Jean, *you've* just got to beat her, cut her down to size.' Oh, it was a nightmare."

When an Olympics is over, most medal winners become mortal again. They suffer an instantaneous fall to ordinariness, a reverse Cinderella tale. For example, Evelyne Hall's husband and mother had driven to Los Angeles from Chicago to see her win her silver medal. The night the Olympics ended they were all invited to a lavish party at Pickfair, the estate of Mary Pickford and Douglas Fairbanks. Unfortunately Evelyne's paid stay at the Chapman Park Hotel was over.

They did not have enough money to stay in L.A. for even one more night and instead of frolicking at Pickfair, they left for home in a car that a Chicago finance company had informed Evelyne (by collect telegram) was going to be repossessed.

And Jean Shiley? The United States Olympic Committee gave this gold medalist a train ticket home to Philadelphia. Instead of using it to ride home in comfort, Jean cashed it in and bought a cheap bus ticket. "I had no money at all and I wanted to buy my family some gifts, some little souvenirs," she said. "I couldn't afford it unless I went home by bus. I sat up all the way, it seemed like ten thousand miles, it took forever."

And Babe Didrikson? She had performed at the Games as much under the aegis of Employers Casualty as of the U.S. Olympic Committee. There was no worry of repossessed cars, no need to nurse nickels by cashing in train tickets. Babe was, in her way, an arm of American Big Business and thus she was treated more like an important executive than a mere Olympian. The insurance company put her on an airliner for the flight home to Texas and not only did the police department band play "Hail to the Chief" when she disembarked in Dallas, but the city fire chief was there, grinning and sweating and bowing before her, offering her the place of honor in his gleaming red limousine. The tonneau was brimming with red roses when Babe climbed into it. She raised her arms and clenched her hands in her gesture of Olympic victory. Members of the Golden Cyclones formed an honor guard at each side of the car. Her family – Mama, Papa, older brother Ole and, of course, shy, pretty Lillie – were there. Lillie had beamed up at Babe through tears, and suddenly Babe yelled, "Come on up here! Come on!" Lillie's eyes once again filled with tears when she recalled that momentous morning: "Oh, I got *up* there with her, and there were roses all over us, all *over* us. It was such a time with

Babe there. I cried, we was so happy in all them roses. I didn't know if I should be there, but Babe said it was okay. Because I was with *her*.

"My mama and my papa and I had ridden up to Dallas in my brother's car with a rumble seat. We was so dirty and so *sweaty* when we finally found th' landin' field. We had two flat tires on the way there and the big shots, they was all lookin' at us country folks, but we didn't care. Babe didn't care. We had our parade through Dallas – confetti and scrap paper fallin' on the cars. At the Adolphus Hotel, they had it full of flowers and beautiful lights for lunch. Oh my. My mama, she couldn't believe where she was. She could hardly speak English, you know, and she kept sayin' she couldn't believe how her baby girl had done all she done. After the lunch, my mama she walked out of the Adolphus carrying a napkin from the table. She was so ashamed – it was a big white ol' napkin – and she was so embarrassed, she wanted to take it right back in, but they said, 'No, Miz Didriksen, keep it, you keep it for a memento.'

"My mama, she did. She took it home to Beaumont and she washed it and ironed it and she kept it folded up in a drawer till the day she died." Lillie paused, remembering that golden Olympic day, and she said: "Babe had to buy us some tires to get us back home to Beaumont that day, did you know that?"

The Dallas festivities lasted two days, then Babe once again boarded an airplane and flew home to Beaumont. Few had heard of her when she left thirty months earlier to join the Golden Cyclones, now she was a goddess. It was like the Fourth of July; an emergency call was to bring in the high school band from summer vacation. The Beaumont *Journal* reported the preparations: "A siren is being placed on the Stinson cabin plane in which she will ride and on its arrival tomorrow, it will circle over the city several times with the siren wide open. This will signal the whistles of the city to cut loose and the official welcome will begin." Thousands came to greet her. An honor guard of members of the Miss Royal Purple high school teams she had played for marched in front of the Beaumont fire chief's car. Babe was given the keys to the city of Beaumont, the mayor spoke, the president of the Kiwanas club spoke. The high school principal, E. C. McDonald, noted that the mark on her school records that merely said "withdrew, Feb. 14, 1930" should be now revised to say, "Left school to be world's greatest athlete." And Tiny Scurlock assured the town, "She's the same swell kid she used to be."

Chapter
9

During the summer of 1932 Babe had captivated not only the hometown folks but the kings of sportswriting – Westbrook Pegler, Paul Gallico, Damon Runyon, Braven Dyer, Frank Menke and Grantland Rice. When the Games were over, Rice, her greatest fan, summarized her achievements, by rhapsodizing:

She is an incredible human being. She is beyond all belief until you see her perform. Then you finally understand that you are looking at the most flawless section of muscle harmony, of complete mental and physical coordination the world of sport has ever known. This may seem to be a wild statement, yet it happens to be 100 per cent true. There is only one Babe Didrikson and there has never been another in her class – even close to her class.

Rice not only anointed Babe as the Ultimate Amazon – the greatest woman athlete – but as the *greatest athlete of all mankind for all time.* After this adulation what could Babe do for an encore? Could she make something of lasting value out of her celebrity? There were bad omens in the immediate past. America tended to treat its heroes like popes at the apex of their fame, but it was usually a fleeting, fickle homage and the rewards were largely ceremonial. Often around the corner from the ticker tape parade lay obscurity, even poverty.

A case in point was Gertrude Ederle. After her successful English Channel crossing she received a public reception that exceeded Babe's. Indeed, Ederle's star rose higher – and then fell farther – than any other female celebrity in those star-crazy times. On August 6, 1926, she set out to swim the English Channel – thirty-three miles from Cape Gris to Dover. The event was covered like a queen's coronation. W. O. McGeehan dramatically synopsized the importance of Trudy's attempt: "I felt that I would sooner be in that tug the day she starts than at the ringside of the greatest fight or at the arena of the greatest game in the world, for this, in my opinion, is to be the greatest sports story in the world."

Trudy covered the distance in the fantastic time of fourteen hours, thirty-one minutes. She smashed the men's record for the distance by more than two hours. She was hailed as "The Grease Smeared Venus," as "Queen of the Waves," and even President Coolidge became relatively effusive and referred to her as "America's Best Girl." Though she was only nineteen, her biography was serialized in the newspapers in microscopic detail. She was a phenomenon.

In New York her reception dwarfed the greeting for Sergeant Alvin York and other heroes of World War I. Not until Lindbergh flew the Atlantic a year later was there a public celebration to match Trudy Ederle's. She arrived in New York harbor on the S.S. *Berengaria* to a cacophony of tug whistles, low buzzing planes and streams of water spouting from fire boats. She rode up Broadway in a ticker tape snowstorm. Two million people crowded the curbs to see her. Mayor Jimmy Walker presented her with a scroll on the steps of city hall. Governor Grover Whalen spoke. President Coolidge sent a telegram.

The night after her return she was mobbed at the Ziegfeld *Follies* and Mayor Walker was annoyed because his "finest" couldn't control the crowd. A thousand guests came to a banquet for her at the Commodore Hotel. Trudy was besieged by movie, stage and commercial offers totalling $900,000. She received hundreds of marriage proposals, and a pair of song-writers did a quickie about it: *"You're such a cutie, you're just as sweet as tutti-frutti, Trudy, who'll be the lucky fellow."* Throughout 1927 she toured American vaudeville houses and made as much as $5,000 a week. A similar tour of Europe was arranged and Trudy had a huge collapsible swimming tank built for the trip. But the strain of doing five and six performances a day was too much. She suffered a nervous breakdown. The trip to Europe was cancelled and Trudy Ederle dropped out of the headlines. In 1935 Westbrook Pegler wrote: "The English Channel swim has been abandoned as a sports event [but] for a whole summer in 1926 the Channel swim occupied about the same importance and the same position in the papers that are now commanded by wars and persecutions. . . . Trudy herself has become a forgotten woman in the city which once buried itself knee deep in ticker tape and torn phone books to welcome her home."

In 1939 she popped back into public view when she swam in Billy Rose's Aquacade in the New York World's Fair with Eleanor Holm and three hundred other show girls. During World War II she worked as an aircraft instrument technician at LaGuardia Airport. In 1975 she was living in an apartment in Queens, childless and unmarried, unknown even to her neighbors. She once said, "Don't write any sob stories about me. I'm not a millionairess but I'm comfortable." When a reporter asked if she felt the world had given her a brushoff, Trudy declared, "I would be stupid if I hadn't realized that people couldn't stand forever on street corners playing brass bands. It doesn't really matter if they've forgotten me, I haven't forgotten them."

In the afterglow of the Olympics Babe Didrikson too knew what it was like to be knee deep in ticker tape and roses; she was one of the most famous people in America. Newspaper reporters followed her every move, printing almost any weird item that might involve her. There were reports of fabulous movie contracts, of high-priced offers to become a bullfighter in Mexico, to be a fashion model in London, to be a professional basketball player for $65,000 a year. These things were absurd, but Babe was so famous that anything about her made news. At one point in 1933, Babe was in Los Angeles and met Amelia Earhart for the first time. Although Miss Earhart had achieved enormous publicity in 1928 when she became the first woman to cross the Atlantic in an airplane, she actually pleaded with Babe to accompany her on one of her long-distance flights (not the fatal one of 1937) because she felt Babe's fame would add luster to the attempt.

This was the grand apex of fame at which Babe existed for a brief time after the Games. She sailed high on her Whatta Gal momentum, a dazzling comet. But not for long. Scarcely twenty-four months after the Tenth Olympiad was over, a column appeared in the New York *Evening Post.* The headline said:

FAMOUS WOMAN
ATHLETE PITCHES FOR
WHISKER TEAM

The reporter wrote:

At an age when most people are wondering when the first break is going to come Mildred Didrikson is one of our most illustrious has-beens. At present she is touring with the House of David baseball team. You know, the boys with the whiskers. Not that whiskered men are such wonderful baseball players, but it's remarkable to see them playing at all. The same is true of the Babe. She goes in to pitch a few innings before the regular pitcher comes on. It's just a stunt that goes over in the tanktowns.

It was probably inevitable under any circumstances, but Babe's fall from the headlines and hymns of Grantland Rice to the obscurity of the back roads of America specifically began when the A.A.U. questioned her amateur status in November 1932. The object of suspicion was a red Dodge coupe she got that fall, an $835 car. At the time, Babe was back working as a stenographer with Employers Casualty, reportedly making only $90 a month. She said she bought the car without a down payment and had arranged payments of $69 a month – which left her $5.25 a week to live on. That sounded suspicious enough to raise questions about whether the car was an illegal gift. However, it was not until her photograph and name appeared in a Dodge advertisement that the A.A.U. charged she had violated her amateur status. Without checking beyond the fact of the ad, the A.A.U. declared Babe suspended indefinitely from competition. (She had been planning to play basketball with the Golden Cyclones again.) Secretary Dan Ferris telegraphed Babe that she would remain persona non grata until she proved "beyond a doubt" that the endorsement was not due to "any act of omission or commission" on her part. It was a clear-cut case of being guilty until proven innocent. Babe declared that the charge against her was all "a bunch of hooey" and wired Ferris saying, "I positively did not give anyone authority to use my name or picture in any advertising matter." E. Gordon Perry, the Dodge dealer who sold her the car, chimed in that Babe had not been paid a penny. He said, "Her praise of this car came from her voluntarily. We passed on to the home office her praise of the car, just as we did many others. Miss Didrikson being a world figure in athletics, naturally attracted more attention than others. Her opinion of the new model car was spontaneous and enthusiastic."

Enthusiastic, yes, but spontaneous? The ad copy, represented as Babe's unexpurgated glorification of the Dodge coupe, read: "Speed – unyielding strength – enduring stamina – that's the stuff that makes real champions, whether they're in the athletic arena or in the world of automobiles." No one from the South End of Beaumont ever uttered such words. Telegrams flashed back and forth between Babe and the A.A.U. for a few days. At last E. Gordon Perry produced a letter he had written to the advertising agency that had produced the ad, proving Babe had no idea her name and photo were being used. Stiffly the A.A.U. backed down and reinstated Babe as an amateur. There was no apology.

Babe was quoted in an interview: "Not until this last weekend did I realize what a terrifying business it is to maintain one's self as a member in good standing in the A.A.U. Being an athlete and being a member of the A.A.U. are two quite different things. I'm not sure which is the more difficult. I am amazed to discover that there are some 350 pages of regulations and do's and don'ts. What a wonder it is that nothing ever happened before – and that any one can continue to be all square with the A.A.U."

After this rather typical A.A.U. flap Babe professed to be delighted that her suspension was lifted, and with her older sister Esther she left Dallas on a train bound for Chicago. At St. Louis, a reporter for the Associated Press found her in the railroad station. He wrote, "Miss Didrikson has turned camera shy. It actually took coaxing to persuade her to pose for a picture, and she did so only after scrutinizing the background for advertising signs. Finding nothing which might lead to complications, she posed willingly."

Her train reached Chicago on the day before Christmas, 1932. Somehow she managed to evade the press and drop out of sight. Reporters were looking for her all over town to question her about her plans. Finally someone found her in a pool hall in the Chicago Loop. She was reluctant to speak, but she did say that she had decided to hire a manager, a fellow named George P. Emerson. Reporters questioned Emerson about Babe's plans; he was reticent. Then, on Christmas Day, Babe announced that she had contracts for three different ventures – to make "sporting shorts" for the movies (the studio was unnamed). Babe said, "So far, I have three jobs – all of them good ones, all of them dignified. Endorsing is not on the list, nor will it be."

This was vague. A day or two later, Babe spoke to a *Time* magazine correspondent and added a confusing new set of possibilities for her future: "Just by way of keeping myself in training, I am seriously considering taking up long distance swimming in a big way," she said. "It is one branch of athletics I have not specialized in before. But I realize that I am too light in weight to withstand the gruelling endurance test of a long distance swim. I want to swim around Manhattan Island then do both the English Channel and the Hellespont. That means I'll have to put on some extra poundage. I have already doubled my food intake. My friends say I'm sure to lose my slim figure, but if I do I'm sure to get it back again. I've done more difficult things."

A day or so after that, Babe and Esther suddenly appeared in Detroit – at the Auto Show. In a fine and ironic twist of promotional gimmickry she had been contracted by the Chrysler Corporation to promote openly the same controversial Dodge coupe which had caused her suspension. She appeared daily at a display booth featuring the car, signed autographs, shilled for Dodge and played her harmonica. It turned out that her "agent," George Emerson, was an executive with the advertising agency that handled the Dodge account – and produced the ad that starred Babe.

When the Detroit show was over, Emerson booked Babe for a stint on the RKO vaudeville circuit and she opened at the Palace Theater in Chicago. She was given star billing. Her name went up in light-bulb letters four feet high, above the billing for Fifi D'Orsay, a singer and movie actress who was appearing in person at the Paramount and was also starring with Zasu Pitts in the feature movie – *They Just Had to Get Married* (Spicy Screen Fun!). Not only was top billing Babe's, so was the star's dressing room. Fifi was understandably miffed, yet when Babe offered her the star's room, Fifi cried out, "How sweet of you dahling! But I wouldn't *dream* of it."

Babe's act was timed for eighteen minutes. She was teamed with a piano player and mimic named George Libbey. It was as bizarre a public performance as any Olympic hero has ever made (Jesse Owens's running races against horses may rival it). Her partner Libbey warmed up the audience with imitations of Eddie Cantor and a couple of tunes on the old 88. Then Babe pranced down the theater aisle from the lobby. She was wearing a Panama hat, a green knee-length jacket, high-heeled Spectators. She sang a song, "I'm Fit as a Fiddle and Ready for Love," adding one of Bing Crosby's patented baritone *boo-boo-boo-boos,* which always brought the house down. The song finished, she sat down, took off her high heels, tied on a pair of rubber-soled track shoes, stood up and swept off her coat to reveal a red, white and blue jacket and silk satin shorts. A treadmill began churning on the stage; it was set in front of a black velvet backdrop with a large clock attached. The clock began running and Babe began jogging on the treadmill, faster, faster, faster. The clock showed her speed. Soon, another person began running on another treadmill, and the climax of the act came when Babe rushed ahead on her treadmill and burst through the tape – the winner! She then hit several plastic golf balls into the audience and wound up her act playing songs on her harmonica, including "Jackass Blues," "When Irish Eyes Are Smiling" and "Begin the Beguine."

She was a hit. There were lines outside despite the wintry Chicago weather. Audiences called her back for encores, Jack Dempsey came to see her show and loved it. A critic for the Chicago *Tribune* wrote:

Friday afternoon was the Babe's first time behind footlights and the girl from the Lone Star state took the hurdle as gallantly as she ever did on the track. If her heart was thumping from the dread disease of stagefright, it wasn't apparent from the audience. Babe sings a song over the "mike", and then goes into her equivalent of a dance. Mildred ends her turn by playing a harmonica with no mean skill.

Weird though most of her act was, Babe Didrikson was indeed a remarkable harmonica player. She had learned as a child on a 35-cent mouth organ, imitating the trills and chords of a Texas radio performer named Castor Oil Clarence. She developed a spectacular imitation of a steam locomotive leaving a railroad station, replete with puffing, steam, shrieking wheels and hooting whistles. Her playing was so accomplished that when one listens to her recordings, she sounds as if two or three people were performing together.

After a week in Chicago, there was discussion about Babe joining the RKO vaudeville circuit at fees reported to be $2,500 a week, but Babe turned it down. "I don't want the money if I have to make it this way," she told her sister. "I want to live my life outdoors. I want to play golf." It is surprising that someone as attuned to money as

Babe would reject such a prosperous offer, but she left Chicago for New York. Her direction seemed aimless and her future was certainly in doubt. She was a professional all right, but a professional what? In New York, Arthur Daley of the *Times* visited her at the Biltmore Hotel and reported:

The Texas lass arrived in town yesterday where she will stay for a couple of weeks while various contracts are being negotiated. Babe ("Don't-Call-Me-Mildred") Didrikson will leave those little details of her new professional career to her manager, George P. Emerson, and to her sister, Mrs. Esther Elam. As for herself, she will keep in training while waiting for some pecuniary reason for putting her manifold talents to some use.

Pecuniary reasons were not easy to find. Babe spoke to Daley about starting a professional women's basketball team in New York, about coaching a girls' track team, about playing baseball perhaps ("I like shortstop best, because I like to scoop 'em up"). It was a strange, jumpy interview. At one point she fixed Daley with a scowl and snapped, "Say, you aren't the fellow who took pictures of my feet out in Jersey a couple of years ago?" Daley said he was not. In the next breath she said: "Don't ask me whether or not I'm going to get married. That is the first question women reporters ask. And that is why I hate those darn old women reporters." Her sister gasped at this and Babe said, "I don't care. I told them when they were here." She told Daley that she hoped to meet Babe Ruth at McGovern's gymnasium the next morning. "I'd love to be able to spar a bit with him," she explained. "I never met the Babe, but, gee, I'd like to put on the gloves with him for a while. I hope they have a punching bag over there. Boy, how I can punch that bag!" And so it went. Daley wrote sadly, "Miss Didrikson is probably the most naive athlete ever to turn professional. Just what form of professionalism she will engage in is somewhat vague."

Later Babe called a press conference and again said she wanted to spar with Babe Ruth at McGovern's. The next morning she turned up there, but alas Babe Ruth did not.

She was not fazed. She had once told Tiny Scurlock, "Give me a big city. There are more people to please, more places to go. I wouldn't be afraid even in New York City." A couple of days later, she played in her first game of professional basketball. This occurred in the Bushwick section of Brooklyn, in an old neighborhood dance paladium called Arcadia Hall. The place was jammed with two thousand raucous fans, mostly from the neighborhood. The hall was a gaudy old joint, lined with Ionic columns of livid green with gold trim; it soon filled with smoke. Babe trotted out onto the dance floor wearing her Olympic track suit, the auditorium rang with Brooklyn clamor: "Yoohoo, Mildred! Heya, take it easy, Mildred! Oh you kid, Mildred!" Jimmy Powers of the *Daily News* wrote:

The Babe grinned, waved back and appeared to enjoy herself immensely. When she fell in the first scrimmage she rose, unaware of an accident that had befallen her pants – she had ripped her blue silken pants wide open. But she arose, shook her head when her trainer signalled for time out, and disdained a change of haberdashery. Soon every one in the hall shouted at her and a regular chant arose, "Hey, Babe your pants is tore." Babe only grinned, chewed her cud of chiclet and continued.

She was playing for the Brooklyn Yankees against a club called the Long Island Ducklings. Babe's team won 19–16 and Babe scored nine points. She was paid $400 for forty minutes of work.

Her next venture was a series of pocket billiard matches against a young lady named Ruth McGinnis. This was a miscalculation on Babe's part, for Miss McGinnis had spent her childhood in her father's pool hall in Honesdale, Pennsylvania. When she was thirteen years old she was matched against Ralph Greenleaf, the touring world champion, and little Ruth ran fifteen balls against him before the startled Greenleaf recovered and defeated her. During preparations for the Didrikson-McGinnis match, a New York writer named Jack Kofoed wrote a hostile but incisive column about the frailty of Babe's new identity as a professional: "Mildred Didrikson has developed a superiority complex of immense proportions," Kofoed said. "Now that she has eschewed the lily white purity of amateurism, and is frankly out for the do-re-mi, Mildred must succeed spectacularly, or the customers won't pay a dime to see her in action." He predicted that Ruth McGinnis would annihilate Babe and added, "It probably will be a good thing for Babe psychologically, even though it won't help the box-office any. She is too sure of herself."

Kofoed was right, Babe was in a vulnerable position with her public. The personality she herself had promoted – and her friends in the press had propagated – was that of a hillbilly braggart, intimidating and infuriating her opponents with outrageous claims of superiority, then frustrating them all the more by doing precisely the impossible things she promised. If there was one cliché that most puritan apostles of sport considered paramount, it was that the only genuinely *worthy* heroes were modest types, bashful, tongue-tied toe-diggers who nearly fainted from the embarrassment of being praised. The 1930s was a time when virtue was the most admired American attribute and there was a simplistic one-dimensional quality to the nation's heroes in general. Decent movie cowboys in white hats like Tom Mix or Buck Jones were at the head of the parade, along with tangible real-life good guys such as J. Edgar Hoover and his sidekick

Melvin Purvis who led the noble G-men of the Federal Bureau of Investigation in almost weekly gun battles with celebrated desperadoes. The most widely read book of 1932–33 was *We,* Charles Lindbergh's unadorned story in which he gave most of the credit for his flight to his airplane.

When Babe was winning, her boastful behavior was allowable, for if there was one thing America appreciated more than virtue it was *results.* But as a loser, her behavior became notably offensive. And, as a loser, her presence in the sporting arena – man's world from time unwritten – attracted a new outburst of male chauvinism. A leader of this hostile crowd was Joe Williams, sports columnist for the New York *World-Telegram.* He had never cared for Babe anyway, and as she went into eclipse he wrote:

Babe simply refuses to accept any concessions to femininity. She is a tomboy grown to womanhood and she used to think she could outjump and outrun any kid in the neighborhood, she didn't have any time for doll playing girls and she hasn't changed much. She talks like Dizzy Dean. And when you get right down to the elementals, she didn't do very much. All the records she made were ordinary. The same year she became the greatest woman athlete in history, a comparative chart shows that she had not equalled one record made by a masculine high school champion of the same period. I recall doing a column on the young lady at the time and suggesting that instead of furthering admiration for her sex she had lowered it. By her championship accomplishments she had merely demonstrated that in athletics women didn't belong, and it would be much better if she and her ilk stayed at home, got themselves prettied up and waited for the phone to ring. If the best woman athlete in the country is not as good as some gawky kid in high school, why waste the effort, why invite the embarrassment of mediocrity, why – well, why not get a seat in the stands and make the big male blokes out there on the cinder track believe you are nuts about them?

Williams's argument was specious; it was like saying that Henry Armstrong or Sugar Ray Robinson were less splendid as boxers because they were too small to defeat heavyweights such as Joe Louis or Rocky Marciano. Williams was merely using a false context in which to compare the quality of Babe's achievements.

As a professional athlete, however, Babe's problem was not proving the worth of the context in which she had competed, it was in finding – or creating – a *new* context in which to exist. Professionalism and female athletes did not mix much in those days: amateur sport offered the only first-class context for women's competition. Indeed, up to that point only a handful of women had even tried to make a living from sports. One of the first and most successful was Annette Kellerman, an Australian swimmer and diver who stunned the world by introducing the one-piece bathing suit in 1907 and later made a nice living performing a diving-board trick called "the standing-sitting dive." In the 1920s the celebrated C. C. "Cash & Carry" Pyle brought French tennis star Suzanne Lenglen to the United States for a tour in which Lenglen played a "stooge" named Mary K. Browne, won every match and went home about $25,000 richer. Helen Hicks, a golfer who won the U.S. title in 1931, became a professional in the early 1930s, played some exhibitions, but made most of her income as a "factory representative."

None of these women pros participated in any kind of *real* competition, for there was none. Their only recourse was to become exhibitionists, who displayed their athletic prowess as a modified circus act. Indeed, to be a great woman athlete and a professional in the 1930s was like being a prima ballerina with only the Rockettes' chorus line to dance in, a great actress with only a traveling cornfield carnival for a stage. It is not remarkably different today: tennis, golf, skiing and bowling, to a lesser extent, offer steady competition and good money to women pros, but there is almost nothing else. A carnival environment still plays a more significant part for women than men – witness Billie Jean King's Barnum-style tennis match with Bobby Riggs, the hokey TV Super Star contest, hot-dog skiing.

Babe did the only thing she could do as a pro: she went on the road as a sideshow attraction.

A promoter in Muscatine, Iowa, named Roy Doan arranged for her to begin traveling during the fall of 1933 with a basketball squad called Babe Didrikson's All Americans. There were four men and two or three women, including Babe; they barnstormed the backroads and country towns, playing against whatever men's basketball teams could be scraped together in the one-horse towns they visited. It was a numbing life of rough-and-tumble basketball games by night and mile after mile of bleak landscape by day. The roads were largely made of spine-jarring washboard gravel and the countryside was endlessly scarred with effects of the Depression. Farmers, their wives and children were harder hit by hard times than anyone and they had come to be wan and weakened people, almost a race unto themselves, standing by the road watching cars go by. Their houses were wind-beaten and gray, their fields lay weedy and unused because many could not afford to buy seed. The Rural Electrification Act had not yet brought power to the nation's outlands and a large section of the country lived in flickering kerosene lamplight or in darkness after sunset. Only thirty percent of the American population lived in cities then; the vast majority were in small towns or farms, and this is the group that Babe's All Americans entertained. They turned out in droves.

Despite the national epidemic of poverty, there seemed to be money for entertainment. There were seventeen thousand movie theaters in the country in 1933 and people crowded to them, often to buy a chance on winning a set of free dishes. Baseball's All-Star game was started and the minor leagues flourished, college football attracted thousands and radio sets were selling at all-time record rates. This juxtaposition of ash-heap poverty and the trappings of affluence led Will Rogers to say, "We are the first nation in the history of the world to go to the poor house in an automobile."

For performing with her All Americans, Babe was paid $1,000 a month, a fantastic income. In the garment shops of New York, women were being paid as little as $2.39 for a fifty-hour week; women working in a pants factory in Manhattan averaged $.06 an hour. Whether Babe was worth that much money is perhaps conjectural, but she was the main attraction, the billboard star of the team, and it was her name – and her name only – that pulled in thousands of small-town gawkers from Thief River Falls, Minnesota, to Fort Plain, New York, during that winter. A teammate of hers on the All Americans, Dick Butzen, Sr., of Fond du Lac, Wisconsin, recalled the five-month odyssey: "Starting in Muscatine, Iowa, we played in Missouri, Kansas, Nebraska, South Dakota, Minnesota, Wisconsin, Illinois, Michigan, Ohio, Pennsylvania, New York, Vermont, Massachusetts, New Hampshire, New Jersey and Connecticut. A total of ninety-one games, winning three-fourths of them and, twice, playing two games on the same day in different towns and winning them both. We traveled in a seven-passenger sedan with a trailer for luggage so we came to know each other very well. Babe was a well-coordinated athlete and though average in size she had a grip that registered higher on a gripping machine than anyone on the team – and we had a six foot, six inch center along. She had her playful side. In an eastern mill town, our hotel was some three hundred feet back from the sidewalk. In a mild snowstorm she built a snowman near the street, using as clothing the long johns I furnished her from my roommate. She was likewise very considerate and insisted whenever she was invited out, that the team received an invitation, too. I realize those five months were not a long time in her fantastic career, but she was a constant surprise. Like, she was paid a thousand dollars a month, which our manager would pay her in cash from gate receipts. She would go to the bank and convert it into a thousand dollar bill and mail it in an envelope to her folks in Beaumont, Texas. After we explained that this was a careless thing to do, she finally made out a money order."

During part of the season, the team had another woman, Virne "Jackie" Mitchell, a short pudgy person from Chattanooga who had spent the previous summer pitching for the House of David baseball team. When the All Americans arrived in St. Louis in December of 1933 for a game against a pickup team that included the St. Louis Brown's catcher Rollie Hemsley, the *Post Dispatch* ran a story on Babe and Jackie:

Both wear their hair in boyish bobbed style, a style in keeping, perhaps with their connection with men's athletics. Babe is wiry and physically hard. Miss Mitchell is of a type opposite to that of her more famous running mate. She is round-faced, and, despite the boyish bob and a leaning toward masculine clothes, is essentially feminine. Her conversational voice is soft. Other members of the team say the girls get along fine together, and if the boys must know it, have no interest in men from a standpoint of other than athletics. "Neither goes for that lovey-dovey stuff," says Harry Laufer, business manager of the team.

Babe completed the basketball tour in March 1934 and went to Florida to appear in some spring training baseball games. This was a gag and a gimmick, of course, but profitable: she usually was paid $200 for a one-inning appearance. One afternoon Connie Mack, manager of the Philadelphia Athletics, had Babe start a game as pitcher against the Brooklyn Dodgers. She struck out the first two batters—"a bit of chivalry: both swung lustily at a pair of strikes each, missing the ball by wide margins," reported the New York *Times*. She then walked one batter, hit another with a pitched ball, and the third hit a hard line drive to Dib Williams, the A's second baseman. He turned it into a triple play – "an honest one," reported the *Times*. A day later, Babe pitched an inning for the St. Louis Cardinals against the Boston Red Sox. She gave up four hits and three runs, and Red Sox Manager Bucky Harris spoke with restrained enthusiasm: "She can handle that old apple with some of the boys." Another day, she pitched for the Cardinals against the Athletics. The Cards' star brothers, Dizzy and Paul Dean, had been joking with Babe and Jimmy Foxx, the A's star slugger, before the game; Dizzy had bet Foxx that "me 'n' Paul 'n' Babe can beat you guys." Babe pitched her inning with Paul Dean in left field and Dizzy shouting encouragement from the dugout. The first three batters got three straight hits, loading the bases. The fourth hit a sharp line drive, which was caught and turned into a double play. Jimmy Foxx stalked to the plate. Babe winked, grinned, wound up and fired the ball which Foxx belted high and far into an orange grove beyond left field. Paul Dean started running at the crack of the bat. He disappeared into the trees at the same time the ball dropped in. A moment later he emerged, carrying one baseball and five oranges in his glove. The umpire had no choice but to call it out number three.

In the late spring, summer and early fall of 1934, Babe toured with the House of David baseball team. They played a killing schedule of two hundred games. Ruth Scurlock, her old teacher and friend from Beaumont, said, "This freakish circus travel she went through after the Olympics was terribly hard on her, physically and emotionally, but spiritually, too. She was really drained. Her father and mother were ill a lot of the time. She must have felt such enormous pressure, and yet she had to go through with those demeaning travels and those ridiculous games."

Babe tried to be as aloof from it all as she could. She recalled: "I was an extra attraction to help them draw crowds. I didn't travel with the team or anything. I hardly even got to know the players. I had my own car, and I had the schedule, and I'd get to whatever ball park they were playing at in time for the game. I'd pitch the first inning, then I'd take off and not see them again until the next town."

Emory Olive, of Eau Claire, Wisconsin, traveled with Babe and the House of David and he recalled: "Babe would pitch one or two innings and we always fixed it beforehand so the other team wouldn't try to score against her. She was not all that good a pitcher, but she could hit. Once at Logan Field in Chicago, we were playing in front of eight, nine thousand people and Babe she hit a line drive and scored, sliding into home in a cloud of dust. She won the game. The score was one to nothing. She was not the only big star on the team. Grover Cleveland Alexander was also with us. He and Babe both got fifteen hundred dollars a month and the rest of us earned three hundred to five hundred dollars. With a crowd Babe, she'd really put out, but if there was no crowd, she wasn't worth a damn. She was quite a girl, she was terrific and could do anything. We wore gray pin stripe uniforms. The only team that could beat us was Satchel Paige's team.

"Babe was given that Dodge after the Olympics, you know, but then she traded it in for a Buick. Once in Beatrice, Nebraska, the Dodge people were all set there, waiting to give her a big welcome when we got there to play and here she drives into town in a *Buick*. Oh, how we laughed. Once after warming up for a game in Yakima, Washington, Babe she was sittin' on a chair along side of the dugout —she'd never sit in the dugout with us — and this woman spectator leans over the rail and yells at her, 'Where are your whiskers?' Without flinchin', Babe she hollers back, 'I'm sittin' on 'em, just like you are!' We all liked her, she was a character and she'd really give you a show. We toured through Canada and she went with us. We drew about five to twelve thousand people every game up there. Grover Cleveland Alexander was the pitcher and the manager. He was the biggest draw, bigger 'n Babe. He was also a heavy drinker. When Babe was with us I never saw her take a drink. She wasn't masculine looking, didn't talk like a man either."

The motive behind Babe's early work as a professional athlete was never in question: there was no real enjoyment, no challenge involved. Only cash. A reporter asked her if she regretted leaving behind the thrills of amateur competition and Babe replied, "I like pro sports and will continue to like them – as long as the money keeps coming in. I guess we all like the money."

She was a sharp, frugal person with money, always on the lookout for a good investment. Her major memory from the first time she met her idol Babe Ruth was that he said to her, "Babe, let me give you some advice. I wish someone had told me this when I was your age. I know you're making money. Put some of it away. Get yourself an annuity." She did exactly that. One luxury she indulged in – always – was big, racy cars. In September 1934, after touring for months with the Babe Didrikson All Americans and the House of David, she wrote Tiny Scurlock: "I said I would not come home again unless I'd made about or not less than $10,000. Well, I'm ready to come – and I have some – I'm really earning it. Although I did spend 18 hundred for a new Buick car, which I think I'll trade for a new LaSalle. They're pretty good looking. Have you seen them?"

With her family, she was endlessly generous. She bought her father a 1933 Dodge. She constantly sent home gifts, Thanksgiving turkeys, Easter baskets. Once, she arranged surprise birthday presents for her beloved mama – a new stove and refrigerator. The appliances were to be installed in the kitchen on Doucette Avenue at the very hour her mother was in the midst of cooking dinner. The dealer and his men crept into the kitchen, hooked up the new stove and the new refrigerator, stealthily removed the old stove and the old icebox, then transferred the steaming pots and the refrigerated food from old to new. "Oh, my mama, she like to have fainted when she come out in the kitchen," recalled Lillie. "Oh, my mama, she seen those new things and she never knew *what* happened. Then she started to cry, then she started to laugh. Then Babe started to laugh, then she started to cry, oh, we was *all* just gushin' tears and laughin' – we was *never* so happy, I guess, as when Babe snuck in my mama's new stove and refrigerator that day." When her father was ill in 1933, Babe paid the bills and she paid when her mother was ill the following year. She bought the construction material for her papa to remodel the second-floor apartment on Doucette Avenue – including, of course, the flashy green fixtures for her "Hollywood bathroom."

Babe often sent Lillie clothing she bought for her public appearances. One day last year, Lillie was paging through her tattered old scrapbook and came upon a photo of Babe leaning over a billiard table in a sleek silky white gown. Lillie pointed at the gown and said, "That there's my weddin' dress. Babe sent it to me and it was like new. Oh, Babe she was always sendin' me clothes – real furs and shoes. I was better dressed 'n anybody in Beaumont when Babe was alive."

Beside the money she made barnstorming, Babe still collected a healthy salary of $300 a month from Employers Casualty whenever she decided to settle in Dallas for a few weeks. Although she was ostensibly just another stenographer there, she had a close relationship with the president of the firm. He used to let her putt on his office carpet and pitch golf balls into the seat of his leather chair during the lunch hour.

Despite the inherent difficulties in being a professional woman athlete, Babe did astonishingly well. In her first three and a half years, she estimated she had earned more than $40,000. This averaged out to an annual salary that was substantially higher than the $8,000 a U.S. Congressman was paid. Yet prosperous though she was, Babe's association with those bands of vagabond ballplayers and the tough veneer she offered the world did nothing to advance her reputation as a respectable – or even an acceptable – model for young women of the day. Nor did her career and personality do anything to help the cause of women's sports. Quite the contrary. Babe herself became a symbol of the negative effects competitive sport could have on women. In Texas, signs were tacked up on bulletin boards in college women's gyms saying DON'T BE A MUSCLE MOLL: the slur was known by all to be directed at Babe. She was used as a kind of bogeywoman by mothers who wished to prevent their budding tomboy daughters from pursuing sports. Dr. Belle Mead Holm, dean of the women's physical education department at Lamar University in Beaumont, grew up in Odessa, Texas in the 1930s and she recalled the way Babe was used as discouragement to sports-oriented girls: "I loved to play softball and I was a bat girl for a team in a league, but I remember my mother would absolutely *weep* over my going to those games. She used to say, 'Please, I don't want you to grow up like the Babe, Belle. Just don't be like the Babe, that's all I ask.' Here I was with all this energy inside me struggling to get out and nowhere to use it. I majored in music in college because it was more acceptable. One day the college president called me in – I just wasn't doing well at all – and he asked me what I really wanted to do. I burst out, 'Play ball!!' Then I broke down and bawled for half an hour in his office. It was so frustrating, I felt so guilty for wanting to play ball. So I know what a pioneer woman Babe was, what a marvel. There were so *many* obstacles – there was that viciousness, that cannibalism among women working against her. There had to be a fierceness in her, a killer instinct of some kind. Babe simply had to have a warlike spirit.

"Sometimes I wonder what might have happened if there had been fashions to make her look attractive. The Babe and the bob – it was bad business, men didn't know how to cut women's hair in those days. Shingled up the back, sideboarded, so ugly. I think Babe was probably embarrassed by her appearance then. But I guess she just felt the package of the athlete was more necessary for her than the look of womanliness. A girl was taught from babyhood that she must always be presentable in order to be marketable. This is less the case today – no makeup, no prissy dress-up stuff, girls are a lot more *natural* and Babe would've been more acceptable these days. Certainly, if Babe had just come out of the nineteen seventy-six Olympics with the reputation she had in nineteen thirty-two, things would be a lot different. She wouldn't have to pitch for the House of David to make her way. She would have opportunities like Micki King has. She could be a great educator, but, of course, Babe's interests didn't lie in academic life, did they? She would get a lot of endorsements. She'd outclass everyone in the Super Stars on TV. She'd be selling lots of soap and furniture polish and she'd be on all the talk shows and maybe a TV commentator. Come to think of it, all of that might not be such a *great* deal better than pitching for the House of David," said Dr. Holm.

Chapter 10

Babe Didrikson had no intention of spending any more time as an itinerant athlete than she absolutely had to. It was only a means to an end, for she had been deadly serious when she announced to her cheering Olympic fans at the Dallas airport in the summer of 1932 that she intended to master the game of golf. It was a most felicitous choice for a number of reasons – not the least of which was that golf had been, for fifty years, a sport more acceptable for women than any other. Partly this was due to the genteel country-club environment in which it was played, rather like a tea party; partly to the fact that the game was never so physically demanding that it caused a lady to be mussed, rather like croquet. Also there seemed to be a trifle less absolute sexism around the golf course, although many clubs did – and still do – treat women as a second class, allowing them no more than a couple of days and inconvenient hours to play. Still, the first recorded incident of women participating in a mixed foursome occurred as early as March 30, 1889, at St. Andrews in Yonkers, New York. The first clubs to actively encourage women to play – the Shinnecock Hills Golf Club on Long Island and the Chicago Golf Club – did so as early as 1891 and 1892 respectively.

The first national tournament for American women was held in

1895 at the Meadow Brook Club in Hempstead, New York. A field of eleven competed, but the costume of the day, as described by a chronicler of the time, seems confining beyond belief:

All were attired in hats and layers of fabric. Long cloth or tweed skirts reached from their waists to their ankles. Underneath was an assortment of petticoats also touching the shoe tops. Blouses with full-length sleeves had starched collars around which ties were draped. Over the blouse it was fashionable to wear a bright colored jacket carrying the club emblem on the breast pocket. On the ladies' feet were heavy shoes, some wore heavy leather boots with metal tackets. On their heads were broad brimmed hats, held in place by hat pins or veils tucked under the chin. Around their waists were heavy leather belts with buckles. . . .

Thus swaddled, draped, shod, cinched, wrapped, cloaked and layered Mrs. Charles Brown won the first U.S. tournament with a score of 132 strokes over eighteen holes.

It is a little-known fact, but the first American woman ever to win a gold medal in the Olympic Games was a golfer – Margaret Abbot of Chicago – who won a golf match associated with the Second Olympiad of 1900 in Paris. Women players increased – and improved – enormously in the early twentieth century; by 1923 there were one hundred and ninety-six entries in the U.S. amateur tournament and the winning score was a commendable eighty-four. By far the finest American golfer in the 1920s was Glenna Collett Vare. She won the national amateur championship six times and was widely known as the female Bobby Jones.

Golf escaped the attacks of Mrs. Hoover's crusading Women's Division (as did other country-club-oriented sports such as tennis and figure skating). A woman golfer carried no social onus at all, there was no talk of commercial exploitation or unseemly vigorous exertion. Golf was, in a word, ladylike.

However, given all those wrappings of gentility and niceness, golf also happened to be a game that even an athlete as wondrously blessed as Babe Didrikson could never master without slavish hard work. Few sports require as much intricate and unnatural adjustment, such infinitesimal control, such subtle muscle relationships, such touch. Unlike bowling, where someone like Babe could stride to the line and do well immediately, or track and field, where her natural speed, strength or stamina could be improved a bit and she could excel, golf demanded countless concentrated hours of practice. Also, Babe had begun at a relatively old age. She was in her late teens before she first touched a club on the snake-infested Beaumont municipal course with her teacher, Beatrice Lytle. She dabbled with the game during her early days with the Cyclones in Dallas, but it was not until she was twenty-one years old – after the Olympics – that she immersed herself completely in learning the game. Master golfers are not unlike concert pianists: it is rare – if not unknown – to find a top tournament player who began the game later than the age of ten.

Fittingly enough, it was at the Olympics that Babe first heard herself labeled a potential golf champion. Naturally, it was her chief fan, Grantland Rice, who said it. On the same afternoon that Babe won her disputed silver medal in the high jump, Granny Rice had been boasting about her to Westbrook Pegler, Paul Gallico, and Braven Dyer, sports editor of the Los Angeles *Times*. Recently, Dyer, seventy-five and retired, recalled: "Granny was always loud in his praise of Babe, and on this day he told all of us in the press box he simply couldn't think of any sport that Babe couldn't master. Pegler was a skeptic and he said, 'What about golf?' Granny said, all right, golf. He sent word down to the field for Babe to come up and see him. She trotted up to the press box immediately. I think Babe probably would have done anything for Granny Rice in those days, it was a case of absolutely mutual admiration. So when Granny said to Babe, 'When do we play golf?' she said. 'Tomorrow.' "

The next day, Pegler, Gallico, Dyer and Rice turned up with Babe at Brentwood Country Club. The Didrikson legend-making machine at the Olympics being what it was, a photographer was there too. Except for the photos of the group, almost everything about the now-famous golf game has come to be a little blurred. Years later in her autobiography Babe declared that she had never played a round of golf before that morning, that she had slipped into the pro shop and begged Olin Dutra to show her how to grip the club before she teed off. This was all strictly grist for the legend. Even her own quotes from newspapers of the day indicated this would be the *eleventh* round of golf in her life. In fact, she had played quite a lot of golf in Dallas.

Perhaps the facts shouldn't matter so much. The important things were that her myth got another edging of gilt *and* that she became enormously encouraged about her game. There was nothing subtle or smooth about her play. She used sheer home-run power on the tees and hit several 250-yard drives. However, she held the club like a baseball bat, she was embarrassing around the greens (she four-putted the first hole) and she was in the deepest rough often. Her score on the first nine was 52 and on the second 43. Had it been anyone else, the morning would probably have been forgotten, but with Babe Didrikson fame begat more fame. The writers pronounced her game a wonder to behold. Granny Rice led them all in the size of his overstatement. "She is the longest hitter women's golf has ever seen," he wrote, "for she has a free, lashing style backed up with championship form and terrific power in strong hands, strong wrists, forearms of steel. She has as fine a swing as either Helen Hicks or

Glenna Collett Vare and it came naturally to her after a few rounds just as everything else comes naturally."

Such magnanimous encouragement could not be ignored and, from then on, Babe had her sights set on becoming a championship golfer. The first concentrated phase of her campaign began in the late winter of 1933, shortly after her first plunge into professionalism. She had saved $1,800 from her appearances at the Detroit Auto Show, the Chicago Palace Theater and in New York. In March, she loaded her beloved Lillie and her mama into the celebrated little red Dodge that had cost her her amateur standing and drove from Beaumont to Los Angeles to become a golfer.

Somehow, the three of them managed to make that $1,800 last for six months while Babe took intensive daily lessons. She could not have afforded this had it not been for the generosity of Stan Kertes, a slim, young driving range pro who volunteered free lessons, free buckets of balls, free practice space for Babe throughout the spring and summer of 1933. In 1975 Kertes was sixty-six years old, a graying, soft-spoken man who had recently retired from professional golf. Gently, he rambled on about Babe – and other subjects: "I was working at this driving range and one night I was giving an exhibition when Babe and her sister Lillie came in and watched. She was a warm and honest person and I liked her right away. She came up to me and said, 'Gee, you swing nice. Can you teach me that?' I knew her, of course, from the Olympics, and I said, 'Sure, we'll start now.' She hit a few for me. Her grip was wrong, she held it like a bat. I had the hardest time getting her to use her fingers on the shaft instead of her fist. Babe used to hit a thousand, fifteen hundred balls every day. Her hands would blister up and bleed. She wore tape on them all the time. Babe would hit eight or ten hours a day. We'd work until eleven o'clock at night. I usually charged ten dollars for six lessons, but I never charged Babe a penny. I was doing all right with my other lessons. I taught lots of movie stars. Al Jolson, Burns and Allen, the Ritz Brothers, the Marx Brothers. I once played a game with Harpo Marx and he wanted me to give him eight feet on every shot. I said, okay, and Harpo brought this string he had measured, exactly eight feet long. The eight feet didn't make any difference on the fairway, but once Harpo was on the green – well, he was putting to a *sixteen-foot hole!* Danny Kaye, Jack Benny, Bob Hope and Bing – Bing's left arm is three inches shorter than his right, you know. I taught Ira Gershwin, Harry James, the Dorsey brothers. In 1934, Harold Lloyd came to me and asked me to teach him golf. He had only three fingers on his right hand; but he was absolutely determined. Once he had decided to learn how to bowl. He made up his mind that he *had* to bowl ten three-hundred games. So he worked until he bowled ten three-hundred games, then he quit. He never bowled one more ball his whole life. That's the way Harold Lloyd was. He came to me and said he'd pay me ten thousand dollars if I could teach him golf well enough to shoot a seventy-one at Rancho Park. I said okay. We went at it. He had a golf course on his estate. He had five greens and nine tees. We used to take movies of Harold Lloyd's swing, day after day. He had his own cameraman, his own developing laboratory, his own projection room. We would watch his swing for hours in his projection room. It took eleven months, then Harold Lloyd shot a seventy-one at Rancho Park. That was it. He never hit another golf ball in his life, not one. It was the same thing with being a Shriner. Harold Lloyd joined, finally got to be Grand Marshal or whatever they have, then he quit for life. Yes, he had only three fingers on his right hand.

"Babe had an obsession something like Harold Lloyd's. People were interested in what she was doing, of course, because of the Olympics. One of the first days I taught her – this was June sixth or seventh, nineteen thirty-three – I called Dorsie L. Dorsie and Paul Lowry, newspapermen, and went out to Lakeside with Babe. They followed her performance. She had a long way to go, of course. She shot a ninety-nine and I shot a sixty-nine. But they were impressed. She had a lot of brains, a lot of imagination about her shots. She'd play any man for money. She played some exhibitions once with John Montague, the famous John Montague – he could hit a bird on the fly with a golf ball. John Montague once played Bing a round of golf using a rake, a shovel and a bat; he could hit a golf ball three hundred and forty yards with a bat. There were lots of characters around here then. Shaggy Wolford; Three-Iron Gates – Ward Gates – could shoot a sixty-eight with a three-iron. They liked to play with this construction guy named Irving King. They beat Irving King out of three thousand dollars on an average every day. They'd give Irving thirty-six strokes on eighteen holes and he'd lose. I once gave Irving sixty strokes over eighteen holes. He lost.

"Babe liked to play for money, too. She liked money. Once in nineteen fifty-four she told me that she had made nine hundred and eighty-five thousand dollars in her life. And she planned to make one million. I'm sure she did. We remained close friends all her life. Once when she was playing in the Tam O'Shanter at George May's course outside Chicago, I was working at a club near there. She was ten shots behind after the second round and George called me and said, 'Stan, you've got to help her.' They drove over and we worked from two P.M. to six P.M. Her grip was turned too much. She was lunging at the ball. We worked on these things. She went back and she won the Tam that year."

Stan Kertes was Babe's first serious golf teacher. She also took formal lessons from George Aulbach in Dallas and Tommy Armour in Chicago, and she did practice obsessively, hitting thousands of balls every week she was not on the road barnstorming. In November 1934 she decided to enter her first golf tournament, the Fort Worth Women's Invitational. She played an eighteen-hole qualifying round, made a scorching score and her name was in headlines again:

Wonder Girl Debuts
In Tournament Golf:
Turns in 77 Score

However, she lost in the first round of match play and went home to Dallas to practice some more. Her goal was to play in the Texas Women's Amateur Championship in the spring of 1935. The hours she put in practicing were endless, a stoic, relentless campaign of hard labor that was almost fanatic. As much as her magnificent physique, Babe's hypnotic devotion to work and her absolute single-mindedness of purpose were responsible for her success at golf. Gene Sarazen spent two months with her at one point touring the country, and he was astonished by her devout commitment to perfecting her game. He said, "I only know of one golfer who practiced more than Babe and that was Ben Hogan."

In April 1935, she decided she was ready to play the best women golfers in Texas and she submitted her entry for the state championship. It was not immediately accepted – some question about the legitimacy of her country-club membership, it was said. But that was not the real problem: Babe had come from nothing, from nowhere, and now she was presumptuous enough to try to scale the walls of Texas country-club society. The South End of Beaumont offered no credentials, no blue-ribbon pedigree, certainly no family wealth that would make Babe truly presentable. Members of the Texas Women's Golf Association snubbed her and complained about her lack of "social status." One member, Peggy Chandler, who had been a finalist in the state tournament for three consecutive years, declared: "We really don't need any truck driver's daughters in this tournament." But they could not keep Babe out because she did have a Beaumont Country Club membership in good standing.

So she arrived at River Oaks Country Club in Houston – and the day before the tournament she received her official welcome to the ranks of Texas women's golf. A driving contest had been scheduled and Babe entered it with enthusiasm. As soon as she did, several women ostentatiously withdrew. They implied that she was too manly, too muscular to engage in competition with their frail ilk. Stung, Babe purposely dubbed drive after drive with an exaggerated girlish swing. Then she hit one with her powerhouse swing and it flew out over two hundred and fifty yards and won the contest. When the event was over, she stayed on the tee and pounded out three or four dozen balls, all of them going more than two hundred and fifty yards. Caddies and a few dozen spectators cheered lustily.

The tournament involved match play between the top thirty-two qualifiers. Babe qualified with an 84. Peggy Chandler had scored the medal qualifying round, a 79. Babe won her first match six up with five holes to play. She won the second eight up with six to go. And she won the third three and two. Now she was in the semifinals. She was to play Mrs. R. E. Winger of Fort Worth. The weather was melancholy, it rained intermittently. After the first nine holes, Babe was two up. A downpour hit the course and the players waited a couple of hours in the clubhouse, then started again on the tenth hole. Babe lost a stroke, then another on the fifteenth hole. The match was even; Babe and Mrs. Winger halved the next two holes, and went into the last hole with the match tied. Rain began to spit down lightly as they teed off. Babe hit a typical shot – long but crooked. It landed in trees off to the right. Mrs. Winger's drive was straight, but not far. Babe recovered from the rough and both were on the green in three. Babe's putt was about twenty feet, Mrs. Winger's about a yard longer. The green was soaked, puddled here and there. Mrs. Winger putted; the ball stopped at the edge of the hole, less than an inch from dropping. She had a five. Babe putted, uphill; she whacked the ball hard. It spurted water all the way up the green, slowed as it approached the cup, seemed to stop at the lip – and dropped in.

The Associated Press reported the occasion with uncharacteristic passion: "Some women cried over the dramatic finish. Men hollered. Babe smiled and walked off the green – still America's wonder girl athlete and probably the most promising woman golf player in the United States." The writer warned, however, that Babe probably could not win the next day, for her opponent was a superb golfer, very experienced in tournament tests, in fact the one-two finisher for the past three seasons. She was Peggy Chandler, the qualifying medalist and declared enemy of all "truck drivers' daughters" in Texas golf tournaments.

The drama, as well as the symbolism, was pure 1930s B-movie material: the underdog, a scruffy, honest, poor girl, versus the favorite, a snobbish, polished, rich woman. A gallery of several hundred turned up for the match. It was to be played over thirty-six holes; the course was still spongy. Babe started as if she were guided by angels. She scored an eagle three on the first hole; the veteran Mrs. Chandler took a six. Babe's game remained supernaturally hot: after twelve holes she was five strokes up. An unbeatable lead? No. Babe began hitting her drives in long loops that ended up amid trees and brush, she missed easy putts, dubbed trap shots. Incredibly, Mrs. Chandler won *six* consecutive holes. She went one up at the eighteenth, then won two more; going into the eighth hole of the second round, Mrs. Chandler led by three strokes. An unbeatable lead? Certainly it would seem so for one so accustomed to tournament pressure. But Babe was relentless. Her game settled down again. She won a hole here, a hole there. As they drove on the sixteenth hole of the second round, they were even again.

This was the thirty-fourth hole of the match. Babe hit a two-hundred-and-fifty-yard drive way ahead of Mrs. Chandler's, but it landed in a ditch. Chandler came up short of the green. Babe belted a three-iron that flew far beyond the green and rolled to a stop in a wheel rut containing an inch of water. The top of the ball was just visible. Mrs. Chandler chipped up within two feet of the cup, a certain birdie. Babe studied her shot for a while, then took a sand wedge and swung. The ball leaped out in a splatter of mud and water. It bounced on the green, slowed immediately with fine backspin, then rolled, rolled, rolled *into the hole!* An eagle three! There was a roar, a burst of applause, whistles from the gallery. People rushed to congratulate Babe. Someone knocked her down in the mud.

Such pure penny-dreadful heroics were not to be denied. Babe and Chandler halved the thirty-fifth hole. Then Babe won the thirty-sixth to take the women's championship of Texas, two up. Many women in the Texas Golf Association were stricken by this turn of events, but Babe's old Whatta Gal fans were delighted to find her back in the limelight. Paul Gallico wrote a congratulatory, but oddly denigrating column. "I wrote a few years ago that when the Babe learned a little more golf and grooved her swing, steadied herself and learned how to approach the putt, she would raise hell with the average competing ladies by her wholly masculine aggressiveness and pugnacity," he said. "Knowing Babe as I do, I can well imagine her swaggering down to her ball, saying, 'Reckon Ah'll hyev ta sink this-a one.' " He marveled that she had beaten such a fine golfer as Peggy Chandler and said,

"Maybe Mildred was wearing her hat perched on the top of her head as she sometimes does, outraging Peg's esthetic sensibilities. Peggy is one of the few lady golfers I know of who knows how to dress. Or maybe it was Mrs. Chandler's neat and feminine clothing that made Didrikson mad. The Texas Babe seems to be working out a lifelong vendetta on sissy girls."

Grantland Rice came through with a predictable tribute. He penned one of his trademarked bits of locker-door doggerel:

> *From the high jump of Olympic fame,*
> *The hurdles and the rest,*
> *The javelin that flashed its flame*
> *On by the record test—*
> *The Texas Babe now shifts the scene*
> *Where slashing drives are far*
> *Where spoon shots find the distant green*
> *To break the back of par.*

Now, if this whole episode had really been part of a B-movie scenario, it would have had a radiant happy ending: Babe Didrikson would have been welcomed into the embrace of Texas women golfers and would have lived happily ever after winning championships, until she retired as a rich and beloved old grand dame who would use her fortune to arrange free golf lessons for truck drivers' daughters. This did not come to pass. Not at all.

The day after she won, someone in the Texas Women's Golf Association complained to the United States Golf Association that Babe was a professional athlete, and since being a pro in one sport infected every other sport, she should be eradicated from amateur ranks. Two days later, Archie M. Reid, chairman of the amateur status committee of the U.S.G.A. concurred, ruling that it was obviously "for the best interest of the game" that Babe Didrikson henceforth be barred from all amateur golf tournaments. The ruling effectively cut her off from every tournament except one – the Western Open. All others were restricted to amateurs.

Now, even though Babe was an unwanted alien in the sleek country of Texas women's golf, she was not a total stranger. When she had entered the Fort Worth Invitational in the fall of 1934, she had been introduced to R. L. and Bertha Bowen of that city, a wealthy and influential couple who had for years been involved in Texas golf. The Bowens lived then – as they still did in 1975 – in a large home in a gracious section of Fort Worth, the rooms of their house subtly decorated with oil paintings, silver and huge antique mirrors. Bertha Bowen was seventy-six, a pleasant, talkative woman with immaculately teased blonde hair. R. L. was also in his late seventies, a tall, stooped, bald man with a delightful smile; he had recently been elected chairman of the board of Community Public Service, a Texas power company. It was to this friendly, influential pair that Babe turned in the spring of 1935 when the U.S.G.A. exiled her from the amateur lists. Bertha Bowen recalled, "We did not know her well, but we had watched when Babe made that long shot from the mud against Peggy Chandler. The gallery just screamed and hollered. It was really something, because in those days you just did not do that on a golf course. You barely even clapped politely, but here was this little gal with all the ability in the world and people just *had* to hoot and holler for her. Oh, she had the world at her feet that day. Then they ruled her a professional. She was beside herself. Babe telephoned me in this little, tiny, timid voice and said, 'Mrs. Bowen, I've just been ruled out of amateur golf. What should I do?' We invited her to the house and when she came we called a lawyer. We sent a telegram to the

U.S.G.A., but there was nothing to be done for it. I was just furious at those people who had been so cutting to her. The fact that she was poor and had no clothes did not mean she had to be ruled a professional."

Bertha Bowen was something of a power in Texas golf; she had had a hand in running the Fort Worth tournament for a number of years. When she discovered that Babe's disqualification was irrevocable, she simply decided that it was time to change the Fort Worth Invitational to the Texas Open, an act that turned it into the second woman's tournament in the country that welcomed professionals. This was done in an openhanded and generous attempt to help Babe Didrikson; the first Texas Open was scheduled for a weekend in October 1935.

In the meantime, there was nothing for Babe to do but play in the Western Open as a professional. She entered there and held a remarkably gracious press conference to announce that she had signed a contract with the Wilson Company to represent their sporting goods line for $5,000 a year and that from now on she would be "a business woman golfer." When a reporter asked her about the precipitant disqualification by the U.S.G.A., Babe spoke gently: "Of course, I was disappointed when they told me I couldn't compete as an amateur, but I admire them for barring me, too. They were big enough to adhere to their rules. And as it all turned out, I'm very happy. My new job thrills me and I know that women's golf has a greater future in this country than men's golf. Golf is a game of coordination, rhythm and grace. Women have this to a much higher degree than men, as dancing shows."

She entered a driving contest before the Western Open; she averaged two hundred sixty yards a shot and smashed one three hundred thirty-six yards with the wind. She shot a splendid 78 medal score in the qualifying round. Unaccountably, she then played poorly in the tournament and lost her match in the quarterfinals. Until the Texas Open she had nowhere to go but back to the hustings and her barnstorming career. This time she took to the road with her new specialty, golf, and a new partner, Gene Sarazen, the muscular, olive-complexioned little man who was the first to win the four major men's championships – the U.S. and British Opens, the P.G.A. and Masters. Along with Walter Hagen and Bobby Jones, Sarazen, then thirty-three, was recognized as one of the finest golfers ever to play the game.

Sarazen and Didrikson toured for two months through New England, the Midwest and the East Coast states in that summer of 1935. In 1975 Sarazen, long ago retired to his vast farm in New Hampshire, recalled his tour with Babe: "I was just out to make a few bucks. It was Depression time. She got a hundred and fifty dollars every day she played and that was a lot of money in those days, but Babe was worth it. I took Sam Snead out on tour with me once and I paid Sam a hundred dollars a match and I *lost* money. With Babe, I easily broke even. She was still a big draw because of the Olympics. People wanted to come out and see this freak from Texas who could play golf, tennis and beat everyone swimming up and down the pool. She had a great outlook on life, she was quick with the needle. We were out in Iowa once and I looked up and said, 'Gee, look at all those steers.' She said, 'Squire, you can't see that far.' She was very congenial and always laughing. She had a gift of playing to the gallery. It just came naturally to her. She was what Lee Trevino is today to the men's tour. She'd turn to me and say, 'What are you using, Squire?' I'd tell her a five-iron and she'd say, 'Well, in that case I got to use a seven.' One day we played at that fancy club outside of Boston – the Myopia Hunt Club – we came in after the round and she promptly challenged the president of the club to a game of tennis. She went out there and played him in her bare feet. Can you imagine playing barefoot at Myopia? She beat him, too. What a character she was.

"We won our matches eight out of ten times, I'd say. She was a real hustler, too, but I never saw her hustle anyone on the golf course. Not then, that came later. Once she was shooting craps in a bar and I tried to get her to leave. She said, 'Squire, don't worry, I can beat these guys. I'm from Texas.'

"She had the natural ability at golf, all right. She had the rhythm, it was just as if she was throwing the javelin. She was very intense and wanted to learn. We'd play an eighteen hole exhibition and then she'd go right back out and practice what she saw. I taught her that sand-iron shot out of a trap; I'd say that trip with me did her a lot of good. She learned all her golf by watching. She'd stand ten feet away from me and watch everything I did. Then she'd go out and practice it for hours. If she couldn't do it, she'd ask me about it. She was a very heady golfer. She was too much show business to ever develop a really sweet swing. She wanted to wallop the ball because that pleased the public.

"I remember one odd thing, she always wanted to be paid off in one-dollar bills. I'd go to write her a check and she'd say, no, she wanted one-dollar bills. Then she'd stack them all up and send them to her bank in Beaumont. Who knows why? I guess she liked the feel of all those dollar bills, I don't know. She did love money."

On that tour, Gene Sarazen and Babe played a match against Horton Smith and the unmatchable Joyce Wethered, the British champion whom most experts still classify as being the best female golfer who ever played the game. Bobby Jones once played a round with Joyce Wethered and declared that he thought she was the best golfer – man *or* woman – he had ever seen. At one point, Joyce Wethered won the English Women's Championship for five straight years – and ran a string of thirty-three consecutive matches in that tournament without a defeat. *The Encyclopedia of Golf* described Joyce Wethered's game this way:

She was perfectly balanced and as poised as a ballerina. The rhythm of her swing, full-pivoted yet giving the impression of economy of movement, was effortless, but it was productive of a clubhead speed and a crispness of stroke that enabled her to out-distance her contemporaries by many yards. She also had a flawless temperament – strung up to the right degree, a touch of humour, the power of pegging away, and above all a legendary power of concentration focused on swinging the club and playing each hole as it came.

For Babe Didrikson, twenty-four years old, champion of Texas and nothing more, playing a head-to-head match with the immortal Miss Wethered should have been the challenge of a lifetime. If Babe could beat her or even come close, her reputation as a golfer would be immeasurably enhanced. Ah, but Babe was Babe. The match was held at Oak Ridge Country Club outside Chicago, and Gene Sarazen recalled: "It was a classic story, I'll tell you. Babe had been using Wilson clubs up till then, all the time. The night before the match the Goldsmith boys went up to Babe and made her a fabulous offer to play with their clubs. Now, this is the night before she is to play the great Joyce Wethered herself. Babe will not have a chance to even try the Goldsmith clubs out, not one chance to hit one golf ball. She liked money, Babe did, and she accepted their offer on the spot. My God, we go out the next day and Joyce shoots a terrific round and Babe plays like she had a seventeen handicap. She couldn't hit the ball at all, we were trounced. She would do anything for a buck, it was like a trout going for a shrimp. Was Babe upset about losing to Joyce? Naw. She said, 'Squire, I got me some do-re-mi,' and she laughed and said, 'Watch me from now on, boy.'"

For the record, the score that day in Chicago was Joyce Wethered 78, Babe Didrikson *88*. In a second match at Meadowbrook that summer, Joyce shot 77, Babe 81. Those were merely exhibitions for Joyce Wethered – nothing to be taken seriously. She was thirty-four years old and had retired from active competition five years earlier. She had married and become Lady Heathcoat Amory. After her American tour, she went back to England and lived in luxury behind clipped hedges of her husband's estate outside London. Gene Sarazen said: "Joyce was the most finished player I ever saw. She could have played on the men's tour, she was that good. But when I was in England, I saw her mansion, and listen, I would have given up golf too."

By the time Babe and Gene Sarazen finished their tour, it was autumn; the first Texas Open was at hand. The Bowens invited Babe to stay at their home during the tournament, and she did. She played poorly, losing in an early round, but that was less important than the new bond of affection that grew between her and the Bowens. After this interlude with them in October 1935, Babe became almost a daughter (the Bowens had lost an infant son in 1930). The Bowens brought a refreshing new atmosphere to Babe's life; they were sensitive, tasteful people, and they introduced the toughened child-woman from Doucette Avenue, this pragmatic "muscle moll," to a whole new dimension of sophistication and gentility. It was never a conscious campaign, never an overt attack, but only a few years with the Bowens produced a major metamorphosis in Babe's view of life and womanhood.

At first she was uncomfortable in their genteel and luxurious home, but soon she felt perfectly at ease. "That monkey," recalled Bertha, "she came for the Open and she ended up staying three weeks with us. She was so poor it was pitiful. She'd have to wash out her one good dress every night. Once we were invited to a formal party during the tournament and we asked Babe to come with us. She hemmed and hawed because she didn't have any clothes. Well, we got her an evening dress and she took one look at it and said, 'I'm not going to wear that naked thing!' She was very, very modest. We had to chase her all over the house before we could get that dress on her. I remember we finally cornered her in the kitchen and forced her into it. Babe ate funny things, too. She'd have a can of pork and beans or an onion sandwich for lunch. She loved strawberry sodas and was forever buying banana chewy candy. When Babe was here in the house with us your life wasn't your own. R. L. took her flying once and she promptly buzzed our house. She didn't want any of that smooth stuff, she wanted to do nip-ups.

"She used her bravado as a defense, but she really had a rough time in those early days of golf. It's hard to break into society when they don't want you. And if you have once been poor, you never really feel that being rich is quite, well, quite *natural*. I was criticized by some of my friends for befriending Babe. They'd ask me, 'Why are you fooling around with *that* girl?' It made me so mad. Sure, Babe could be crude, but around those ladies she was very timid. I don't know how she did it, but Babe never held a grudge about all that. I never heard her say a bad word about anyone. She did want to do things right. She started wearing some of my clothes and then she started to make some of her own golf dresses. She did like to dress up. I took her into Nieman-Marcus. We saw Mr. Marcus and he helped us pick out seven hundred dollars worth of clothes for her."

The Bowens' adoption of Babe was never popular with some of their quasi-aristocratic country-club friends. The women kept sniping at Bertha about Babe, demanding that she put *"that* girl" into a girdle. "We finally decided maybe Babe *should* try a girdle," said Bertha. "So she put one on and went out to play golf one day. I recall her return to the house. The car came screeching to a stop in the driveway. Babe came tearing into the house and she was shouting, 'Goddamn, I'm *chokin'* to death!' She took it off, and she never wore a girdle again, so far as I know." (For years, Babe brought guffaws from galleries by standing on a tee, gazing off down the fairway, then declaring to the crowd, "Well, I'm just gonna have to loosen my girdle and let 'er fly!" It was her primary stock wisecrack, but apparently there really never was a girdle to loosen.)

The transformation in Babe's looks, after only a little of Bertha's cosmetic advice, was stunning indeed. Her friends in the press who had not seen her since the Olympics were astonished. Paul Gallico saw her shortly after she came under the Bowens' wing. He wrote: "I hardly knew Babe Didrikson when I saw her. Hair frizzed and she had a neat little wave in it, parted and prettily combed, a touch of rouge on her cheeks and red on her lips. The tomboy had suddenly grown up. Mildred Ella said to me, 'Ah got tired of being a tomboy, so Ah quit. Ah'm a business woman golfer now, so Ah guess Ah hyev to look th' part.' " Gallico still had her talking like Pansy Yokum, but at least she wasn't Mildred the Muscle Moll anymore. Two years after the Bowens' influence took effect, another old friend, Henry McLemore of the United Press, saw Babe and he was bowled over. He wrote:

Her hair is worn in a soft brown, curly cluster about her face. Her figure is that of a Parisian model. Her tweeds have the casual authority of New Bond Street and her ruby red nails were a creation of Charles of the Ritz. That is the Mildred (Babe) Didrikson of 1937 as I found her today lounging in the cushions of the Hotel Charlotte Harbor sun porch. Honestly, I looked at her twice before I was sure she was the same Babe Didrikson that I had last interviewed at the women's national track and field championship at Newark, N.J. in 1931. The Babe was just a sweat-shirty Texas gal then, ready to begin an athletic career which stamped her as the greatest competitor, man or woman, who ever lived.

Obviously, a more womanly new woman was in the making. The fiercely sheared bob was gone and the vendetta against femininity was at an end. She was twenty-six years old when Henry McLemore declared that her sleeping beauty had been at last awakened. Logically, next came Prince Charming.

Chapter 11

The romantic life of young Babe Didrikson was not exactly snipped from the reels of a Deanna Durbin movie. In high school, no one recalled her ever having a date. No one recalled her ever showing the slightest interest in boys as anything other than opponents to be bested. When she moved to Dallas to work for Employers Casualty, she was no high-flying social butterfly either. Tiny Scurlock wrote in his unofficial biography: "Babe was a bit more social minded in Dallas and went for airings in flivvers. But she had no use for 'sheiks' and they soon learned that." Somewhere along the line, she did learn to dance – indeed she was quite an elegant ballroom dancer. Whether she had any serious beaux at all is problematical. In her autobiography she said, "I had dates and boyfriends from the time when I was working in Dallas. For a while there were two that were fighting each other. I couldn't help getting a kick out of that. I went with one of them for several years." Babe's autobiography, ghostwritten by Harry T. Paxton for a five-part *Saturday Evening Post* series in 1955, is, in part, rather a hokey glossing-over of facts and perhaps this was such an item. Her sister Lillie, who lived with Babe in Dallas as well as Los Angeles during much of the early 1930s, did not recall her ever having a man she saw regularly. However, Babe apparently did have crushes on a few men early in life. Tiny Scurlock recalled that she told him once she "sure did like to be around" a six foot, four inch center who was traveling with the Babe Didrikson All Americans in the winter of 1934. Nothing came of this, for on September 21, 1934, during her vagabond tour with the House of David, she wrote Tiny on stationery from the Majestic Hotel ("Absolutely Fireproof, 200 Rooms – 200 Baths") in St. Louis: "Dear Tiny, I got a letter from home and also a clipping which I will enclose about it being said from Walter Wentchels Column that I was married or going to be – well, he may be right, but I'm not saying a thing. I may be married, but if so it isn't to one of those Whisker boys – I'll guarentee you that – if I am married I am going to let people find out who my husband is." She finished the letter saying, "I wasn't going to write only to tell you that if I am married and anyone wants to knew who he is, they will just have to find out. Your Friend, 'Babe' Didrikson."

At one point, she used to fly into a rage whenever reporters asked her about romance or marriage, but, when Henry McLemore interviewed the sleek and lovely new Babe in January 1937, she was merely coy. McLemore wrote:

Babe is not thinking of getting married. She thought about it last year – in fact, she got within one block of the preacher's house. But – let her explain: "We were just a block away and all of a sudden I said to myself, 'Babe, you better wait awhile,' so I jumped out of the car. It was going about twenty miles an hour and I wrote the fellow a letter of explanation a week later." The fellow (she wouldn't tell his name) is a major league baseball player.

The name of this disappointed suitor remains a sweet mystery to this day. Gene Sarazen also recalled that Babe had a brief but intense crush on the man who directed their golf tour in the summer of 1935.

Ah, but whatever love life had gone before, it was instantly swept aside – or more likely rent asunder – when Babe met the professional wrestler George Zaharias on the first tee of the Los Angeles Open in January 1938. He was gargantuan, a bombastic, jolly fellow, six feet tall and weighing two hundred and twenty-five pounds. Later he would balloon to even larger size, gaining another one hundred and fifty pounds and growing a belly so immense that he could no longer squeeze into trousers with a fifty-two inch waist. Later, Babe would joke, "When I married him, he was a Greek god, now he's nothing but a goddam Greek."

But when she first saw him, George Zaharias was a striking looking fellow with a waist no more than thirty-six inches around, shoulders wide as most doorways, a thick crop of wavy brown hair that was parted in the middle in the style of the day. He had a wide smile, intense dark eyes, strong blunt features. His ears were crushed like cauliflowers from years of wrestling, his nose thick from countless bruises and breaks, and he had hands as big as children's baseball mitts. There was immense vitality in George Zaharias then, a monumental joie de vivre, a vast self-confidence. He was thirty-two years old, famous among millions of wrestling fans, and quite rich. He had climbed a long and arduous stairway to this point from a childhood of desperate deprivation.

George grew up in Pueblo, Colorado, a tough and seamy steel town. The family lived in dismal circumstances in a tiny shack on the prairie. George's sister, Mrs. Joan C. Zavichas, recalled the bleakness of their childhood: "Our parents (Vetoyanis is the family name) settled in Pueblo after their arrival from Greece. In exchange for a one-room adobe house with a dirt floor, they went to work for a rancher, leaving the four of us, ranging from aged nine to a toddler, to fend for ourselves. Two older sisters, Mary and Helen, were married at the time.

The only substance left for us while our parents toiled from sunup to dark was a pot of black coffee and Greek bread. Our parents did not return during the day, and George, being the oldest, was in charge of us. I always remember our being in a starved condition. Any staples that we did have were locked up for fear that we would waste them or spoil them. Our father made two trips to town a year by horse and buggy to purchase a few essentials, so nothing would be wasted. As young as he was, George knew that he had to keep us going day in and day out. Mashing the hard bread in some black coffee, we fed little Tom. One day George came up with the idea of mixing olive oil, vinegar, and salt and pepper in a bowl and beating it with a fork. He then taught us to dip our bread into it, and to this day I can remember how good it tasted."

Later, George was a shoeshine boy and a pool hustler in Pueblo. Then he learned the hat cleaning business from an uncle in Oklahoma City, then he dropped out of school, drifted around the country as a carnival roustabout, eventually winding up down and out in Chicago with one dime in his pocket. He saw a sign outside a gym saying, WRESTLERS WANTED – 1 DOLLAR A DAY. His name then was Theodore Vetoyanis and for his first matches he selected the ring pseudonym "Ted Victory." Later he changed it to George Zaharias. This was the surname of a long-dead relative in Greece and he changed it partly because he did not want to bring scorn to his real family name by having it associated with the dubious work of professional wrestling. And partly, he stopped being "Ted Victory" because he had learned that his own path for fortune in the ring lay not in victory, but in defeat. George played a great craven coward, a classic rotten wrestling villain who fouled, cheated, pulled all manner of dirty tricks on his opponents in the ring. At last, the hero would rise up in righteous anger and pound George Zaharias to mock pulp. At this point George would sob and howl and beg for mercy. He would bawl for help, plead, cringe, tremble, whimper and weep real tears. George wrestled as a crying villain in all parts of the country. He once toured backwaters of the South playing The Carpetbagger while his friend Herman Hickman played The Southern Gentleman. Ultimately, George came to be billed as The Weeping Greek From Cripple Creek (which is forty miles from Pueblo). So convincing was his act that he had the distinction of being selected to participate in the first wrestling match ever to appear on American television. In 1938, at the Ridgewood Grove in Brooklyn, TV technicians carefully daubed The Weeping Greek and his opponent with bright yellow makeup from head to toe so they would show up clearly on camera. The match was broadcast over a radius of one square block; the signal could go no farther than that.

Sid Marks, the security chief at the Horseshoe Draw Poker Club, was one of the myriad cast of characters George Zaharias knew. "I never knew a man living I liked better 'n George Zaharias, except Jim Londos, and I loved him," said Sid Marks. Born in London in 1900, Marks had moved to Los Angeles in the 1920s, where he boxed in clubs, became a stunt man in the movies and finally drifted to the fringes of big-time wrestling where he met George. "Wrestling was big then, nineteen twenty-four, twenty-five," Sid said. "They had just put up Olympic Auditorium then and I used to do announcing outside. There was wrestling every Wednesday, boxing every Tuesday in nineteen twenty-five at the Olympic. George had been a wrestler back east in Denver. He was big in L.A. There are two kinds of wrestlers, see. There are real wrestlers, true-blue athletes who are real good. They could break your arm, they are terrific athletes, they are known as 'shooters.' Shooters never drew crowds too good. Then there were the showmen. The *pretended* they were wrestling, put on a big show. A good showman made many times more money than a good shooter. *Many* times more. George was one of the best of the showmen. He was probably the best villain in the business. George was such a showman they sent for him to wrestle in the Garden in New York. This was the top. That's when George earned his nickname – 'Subway.' Did you know people called him 'Subway'? Everybody in wrestling knows him as 'Subway.' It happened when he was in New York City for the first time, outside the Garden, and he saw all those people goin' down the steps into the ground and he followed them. When they got on a train, George got on, too. He didn't know where he was going, he didn't know where he was. He was supposed to wrestle that night in the Garden. He went down in the subway sometime around noon. He didn't get back until that night, late. They had to delay George's match two hours, I think, in the Garden until he came out of the subway. Everyone knows George as 'Subway' Zaharias.

"He was a great actor, there were no actors like him in wrestling. Famous movie stars used to come to watch him act in the ring. They'd never miss a night that Subway wrestled at the Olympic. Edmund Lowe and Victor McLaglen, Pat O'Brien, Jack Holt, Ralph Bellamy. They'd sit up front so they could get their acting lessons from George, he was that good. Listen, George Zaharias cried real tears. Absolutely real tears. When he got to promoting matches, I used to work with George at Olympic as his right-hand man. When there were beefers, guys who didn't want to do what they were told, George would send me to talk to 'em. Maybe a guy wanted to win instead of lose, you know, so I would go over and say to him, 'You want to *win,* you think? Forget it. Ask yourself another question: do you want to *work?* You do? Then do as you're told to do. Lose.' "

George Zaharias was enormously prosperous at wrestling and

promoting. He made well over $100,000 a year during his best years in the late 1930s and early 1940s. An old friend, Bill Bryant, who operated the California Country Club in Whittier, recalled in 1975: "George used to get fifteen thousand dollars for one night's work sometimes and he wrestled five nights a week. He was tight with his money, but the first time he had any, he bought a farm for his folks back in Pueblo. He was a top headliner, but he never thought he was the best wrestler. He always said he was number two to Jim Londos. Those guys earned their money, those wrestlers. Once, Man Mountain Dean broke George's arm. He was out for six weeks. Then he came back and fought The Mountain again. This time The Mountain threw George into the fourteenth row and broke his leg. But George made a lot of money out of wrestling."

When George and Babe met in 1938, she was living permanently in Los Angeles. She had moved Mama, Papa and Lillie out there about two years before, and they were all living in an apartment near Paramount studios. Babe was practicing her golf game with Stan Kertes, picking up cash here and there with exhibitions and entering whatever few tournaments she could. Her game had improved to the point where she became the first woman to qualify for the Los Angeles Open, a regular men's P.G.A. competition. She said in her book:

I knew I wasn't going to beat the top men pros, but I was still trying to establish myself as the greatest woman golfer. . . . I wasn't the only one who didn't have any business being in it. There were some fellows who were good part-time golfers, but not in a class with the real pros. One was C. Pardee Erdman, a Presbyterian minister who was professor of religion at Occidental College in Los Angeles. . . . Another was George Zaharias. I found out afterwards that he'd done some of his golf playing with Lloyd Mangrum and a couple of other pros. One day when he broke eighty he said as a joke, "Now I'm ready to enter the

Los Angeles Open." And they told him, "Why not? You'll have some fun and it'll be good experience for you."

Babe, the clergyman and the celebrated "weeping behemoth," as he was sometimes called, teed off for the round. The Reverend Erdman beat them both; he shot a 75, George an 80 and Babe an 81. "We kept jokin' with the preacher that maybe he'd just have to up and marry us, we were getting along so well," said George. The two of them dated for dinner that night, played a second round together the next day: neither came close to making the thirty-six hole cut for the rest of the tournament, but they went dancing that night, met again the next day to watch the third round of the Open, went out again that night and then began a series of steady dates that never really stopped. Babe introduced him to Lillie and her mama one night. Lillie recalled: "The day she was gonna bring George home, Babe she said, 'Lillie, fix your hair, we're havin' company tonight.' Then when he come and I opened the door and here I saw that big ol' man standin' there and I thought, 'Lord! Where'd *he* come from!' And my mama she made Norwegian meatballs for dinner. Babe, she didn't fall in love until George come along. But he was *it!*"

George recalled that night, too. "When I got ready to leave, Babe's mother reached up and patted me on the cheek and said, 'My Babe likes you.' Everything was OK with everyone right from the start. After that, I was always looking for her at driving ranges and she'd leave me notes that said, 'Romance was here.' I was wrestling every night. I never took her to the matches. She didn't like them because she thought I might get hurt."

Their affair was searing, sexy almost from the start. They traveled together at times, had an apartment together in St. Louis, enjoyed a sex life that was "red hot," according to stories Babe told her friends later. Once, in the 1940s, Babe was attending a cocktail party with a group of reporters and editors in Los Angeles. One editor who did not know her well approached her rather tentatively and spoke in serious tones: "Tell me, Mrs. Zaharias, of all the records you've broken and all the events you've won, what was the single most thrilling experience of your life?" Without a pause Babe replied, "The first night I slept with George."

Babe had written her old friends Ruth and Tiny Scurlock in Beaumont about having met "someone" she wanted them to meet. She and George arrived in Beaumont together and invited the Scurlocks to dinner at the home of a Greek friend. Ruth Scurlock recalled: "We were so excited when we found out who the 'someone' was. We knew George because he had wrestled in Beaumont many times. Babe had this big ring and she was so delighted. That night, she drank a little more ouzo than she should have and she got a little tipsy. She was slurring her words. George moved right in and took care of her, so fondly and so gently for such a giant. Babe seemed to love that, she seemed to like to play 'the little woman,' to have someone there to protect her and defend her. It was a role she had never played before. She was so happy that night."

George and Babe were married December 23, 1938, in St. Louis, at the home of a wrestling promoter named Tom Packs. Leo Durocher and Ducky Medwick of the St. Louis Cardinals were members of the wedding. Babe wore a blue dress and a blue hat, picked out for her by Durocher's wife. They did not have a honeymoon until the following April when George promoted a golf tour for Babe in Australia. They took a boat there, then went through a grueling exhibition schedule. Babe balked a bit at the rigorous schedule, but George was adamant and she did as he said. They turned a nice profit from the trip. Babe played in New Zealand too, and they spent several weeks in Hawaii on their way home. They were gone six months.

All through their marriage, they were a peripatetic couple. George had what he called "the itchy foot" and he was constantly wedging himself behind the wheel of one of the big new Cadillacs or Buicks he ordered every year (he could never fit his bulk into the front seat of a smaller car) and spinning off for some distant point. He would leave whenever the mood struck – at dawn, midnight, in the middle of a meal. He would drive from Los Angeles to Pueblo – twelve hundred miles through the mountains – as if it were a trip to the corner store. Betty Dodd recalled: "He used to say to Babe, 'I'm goin' to get in the car and just go' and, *bang,* he'd be off. He might be gone three weeks, Babe never knew."

R. L. Bowen said: "George knew someone in every town in the country. He always had an in with someone and he could get anything wholesale – or for nothing. Oh, he was a wheeler-dealer and he had a walrus hide, he was *real* thick skinned. He wasn't welcome everywhere he went, but George was real restless and he went where he wanted to go."

Although Babe loved having a home, doing all the domestic chores from watering rose bushes to washing the dishes, George *had* to have the open road. They owned or rented a number of homes during their marriage – in Los Angeles, Denver, Chicago, Tampa – but none was permanent. Their lives were stamped with this rootlessness, which was caused only partly by the mobile nature of their careers. Babe traveled because of her profession; George went because of a compulsion.

They were a volatile rollicking couple, racing back and forth across the country, consuming huge amounts of champagne and steak, promoting deals ranging from golf clinics for Babe to free tanks of gas.

George gained more and more weight, going over three hundred pounds. Babe did too and at one point weighed one hundred sixty-five pounds. Both were from a world outside the routine of buttoned-up society, both were notably different looking – he with his grizzly-bear size, she with her athlete's swagger, her prominent nose, her tough-guy jaw.

Their affection was intense, constant at first, and George's bordered on the childlike at times. Fred Corcoran recalled an incident in New York: he and George were dining at Al Schacht's restaurant and Babe was playing in the Texas Open. "George kept getting up with this big napkin tucked under his chin and calling people to find out how she did," said Corcoran. "Finally Al Schacht got a report from the Associated Press. He came to our table and said, 'Well, Babe lost but it was real close.' I said, 'How close?' and he said, 'Ten to nine.' I told him, 'Al, you mean ten *and* nine, that's not close, that's the worst defeat of her life.' George stared at us, blinked and walked right out of the restaurant with the napkin still under his chin. I think he cried all night."

Ultimately, George gave up his own career to manage hers and, at times, he missed public recognition. R. L. Bowen recalled, "When Babe was at her zenith, George used to beg her to come stand with him on street corners in Tampa. Poor George, he just wanted to be seen with her."

George was an intelligent, go-getting promoter who handled Babe extremely well. R. L. Bowen said, "In the early days, he was good support for her. He kept her from being exploited. That Dodge car thing wouldn't have happened if George had been managing her." Yet it irked him at times that he had left his limelight and was so dependent on hers. When he felt Babe was too full of herself George would rise up, stick out his barrel chest and say, "Goddammit, Babe, I was a celebrity in my own right — and don't you forget it!" Then he would threaten to drive her and drop her off in a slum neighborhood — "so you don't ever forget where you came from!"

Though he was subtle and effective in the business of Babe, George was a plunger in investment, an eternal promoter of deals. He was in and out of dozens of money-making schemes over the years. Some were successful, such as a tailor-made clothing shop in Beverly Hills, which was patronized by such lights as Charlie Chaplin and Damon Runyon, who used to order ten suits at a time. Some were failures, such as his pouring tens of thousands of dollars into a hopelessly inept professional football team called the San Diego Gunners, a member of the doomed Pacific Coast American League. George also lost money on a rundown Denver hotel he bought, a place of which Babe said after her first tour of the premises: "George, the only way you're going to make a profit on these rooms is to rent them by the hour." One successful venture was a golf course and clubhouse he and Babe bought in Tampa in 1950. They paid $40,000 for it, held it for four years and sold it in the spring of 1954 for $250,000.

George had a nationwide reputation for being thrifty, but when it came to Babe he was uncharacteristically generous. Stan Kertes, her long-time golf teacher in Los Angeles, recalled a revealing incident: "George came to my house late one night. He had been drinking and he went right into my kitchen and threw open the icebox. George took a whole turkey in his hands and ate it, gobbled it down. When he finished the turkey, he said he wanted to take me to see his investment counselor. I objected since it was so late, but George got on the phone, got the fellow out of bed and we went there. He was sitting there in his bathrobe, just out of bed, bleary-eyed. George had lots of property around L.A. then, and he said to this fellow that he wanted to give me a piece of property on Santa Monica Boulevard with six motel units on it. 'Stan, I want you to have it,' he said, 'because you gave Babe those free lessons for all those years. I want to pay you back for that, Stan.' Well, George was in his cups. I finally managed to talk him out of giving it to me. Not long ago George leased it to McDonald's and will get three thousand dollars a month for life from it. I didn't need anything from him or from Babe, but I think he really wanted to give it to me."

One thing George never was able to give Babe that she wanted badly was a baby. She had at least one miscarriage, which left her fairly depressed. She once told Peggy Kirk Bell: "I'd give up every trophy I ever won if I could have a baby." George explained that they had tried to adopt a child once but that the agencies involved would have none of it because the Zahariases were on the road too many weeks a year.

As the years passed, they continued to present a sugarcoated front to the press and the public, but the marriage was turning stormier, and they argued about many things – about George's drinking, about their investments, about divorce. Nevertheless, they never separated permanently. And George's generosity and his promotional talent were such that Babe was able to make an essential and costly switch in her career that could never have been accomplished without him.

Chapter 12

On January 21, 1940, Babe renounced professional golf. She wanted her amateur standing back; there simply wasn't enough work for a female pro. The United States Golf Association had an arcane rule that stated that if she had not been a professional for more than five years, and if she had four letters of endorsement from people prominent in amateur golf and if she stayed away from all forms of playing for pay for three years to come, she would then be deemed pure once more. Three years without pay. By herself Babe had no way of earning a living except through sport – or perhaps stenography. But now there was George. His income was more than enough to carry her – and her totally dependent family – through three fallow years.

Ironically, she spent her payless interim in more prosperous surroundings than she had known in years. She and George temporarily settled in West Los Angeles in a rented duplex with a yard. Babe mowed the lawn, planted rose bushes, bought herself a sewing machine and filled the house with drapes and bedspreads and slip covers she stitched herself. She began taking tennis lessons. Her teacher was Eleanor Tennant, an excellent professional who taught Alice Marble and later Maureen Connolly. Babe went after the sport ferociously, much as she had attacked golf. She played sixteen or seventeen sets a day, wore holes in a pair of socks every other day, in a pair of sneakers once every two weeks or so. Her game was frighteningly powerful though occasionally erratic (some people swear she could smash a ball through the net). Babe played at the Beverly Hills Tennis Club, not far from where George ran his custom-tailor shop. She played for fun there against movie stars like Paul Lukas, John Garfield and Peter Lorre, and she played for blood against some of the best players in the country such as Louise Brough, Pauline Betz and Margaret DuPont.

After eighteen months of concentrated lessons plus Babe's own grimly machined practice sessions, Eleanor Tennant told her it was time to enter a tournament. Babe tried to get into the Southwest championships in the fall of 1941, but she was rejected. Perry Jones, president of the brass-bound United States Lawn Tennis Association, loftily informed her that not only was she not eligible to compete in the U.S.L.T.A. then, she would *never* be eligible. Once she had taken money for performing any sport, she was forever unclean. In the closed minds of the U.S.L.T.A., just as one could not be a little bit pregnant, one could not be a little bit professional. Babe never swung a tennis racket again. She wrote in her autobiography, "Once I knew I could never compete in tournaments, that took the fun out of tennis for me. It's not enough for me just to play. I have to be able to try for championships."

At one point during her layoff, Babe and George went shopping for a bowling alley. The sport was in ascension around the country then, and they examined dozens of alleys around Los Angeles. They decided not to buy one, but Babe became fascinated with the sport. Once more her obsession for perfection took over and she spent hours every night in bowling alleys. She took lessons from several people and she learned to throw a straight powerhouse ball that thundered down the alley like an express freight train. Later she switched to a sharp, swift hook and became one of the best women bowlers in Southern California. One night she and her five-member King's Jewelry team scored a spectacular 2765 for a three-game series in the classy Southern California Major League. Babe's high game for the night was 237. Her average for a season in the Southern California Major League was 170. She even bowled exhibitions (gratis, of course) against first-class stars such as Andy Varipappa and Hank Marino.

Babe also kept her golf game polished to a high sheen by playing a couple of rounds every week. One day in 1940 she shot a 64 at Brentwood Country Club, the best score ever made there by a woman. And several months after she began her U.S.G.A. decontamination period, she entered the 1940 Western Open and the Texas Open – refusing any cash that might be offered. She won them both, and this was widely ballyhooed as Babe's Little Slam, since these were the only tournaments she was eligible for. Surprisingly enough, they were also the only tournaments she had won since she beat Peggy Chandler for the Texas championship five years before.

Although Babe and George were single-mindedly focused on her sports career or on finding profitable investments for his money, the world was rapidly slipping toward hellish times. In 1940, the jackboot armies of Germany had swept through France, Belgium, Holland and occupied them as well as George's and Babe's ancestral homelands: Greece and Norway. President Roosevelt won an unprecedented and controversial third term over the previously unknown Republican lawyer from Indiana, Wendell Willkie. FDR was victorious, at least partly, because the country was reluctant to change leadership at a time when war seemed so imminent. The Battle of Britain produced one of history's most inspired and courageous homeland defenses that year and, whereas a Gallup Poll in May 1940 showed 64 percent of the country was against American aid to England, by December Gallup

When Babe met George Zaharias in 1938, he was a muscular giant, a professional wrestler who sometimes made $15,000 a night. Their wedding was in St. Louis, and Babe wore a hat designed by Leo Durocher's wife.

Their marriage was idyllic for several years; gradually George was transformed from "a Greek god into a goddam Greek," as Babe used to joke. His appetite was gargantuan and, soon, so was he. Ultimately George weighed almost four hundred pounds.

*In 1955 George and Babe built a deluxe home in Tampa. She adored
domestic life, but George was a compulsive traveler. They grew apart in later
years, but they never separated.*

Babe made $500-a-night appearances in major league ballparks, pitching or playing third base during batting practice.

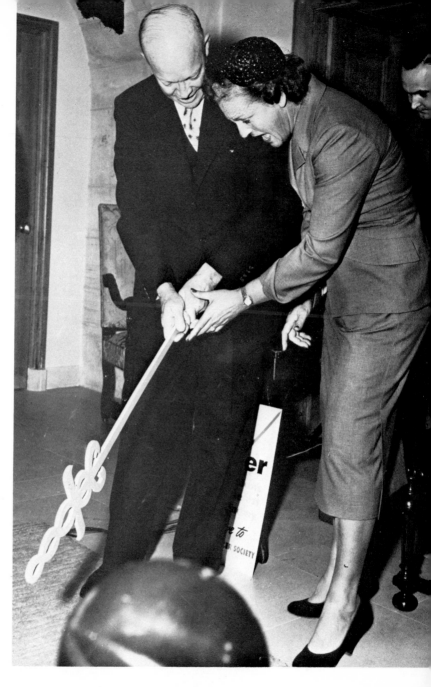

She used to greet President Eisenhower with a cheery: "Hey, Mr. President, how's Mamie's golf?"

Babe was the first American woman to win the British Amateur Championship. Her celebrated blue corduroy "slocks" captivated the Scots, as did her unbuttoned Texas behavior. Always ready to entertain, she performs with golfing friends Polly Riley (left) and Betty Dodd, her protégée in the last years before her death.

Betty Dodd was Babe's constant companion when she was in the worst throes of cancer. Babe's fight against the disease lasted more than three years, but she was cheerful and active until only weeks before she died.

The metamorphosis from the tough young Texan known as Muscle Moll to a vibrant, graceful woman who dominated golf and became a millionaire required enormous courage as well as almost superhuman athletic talent. There will never be another Babe.

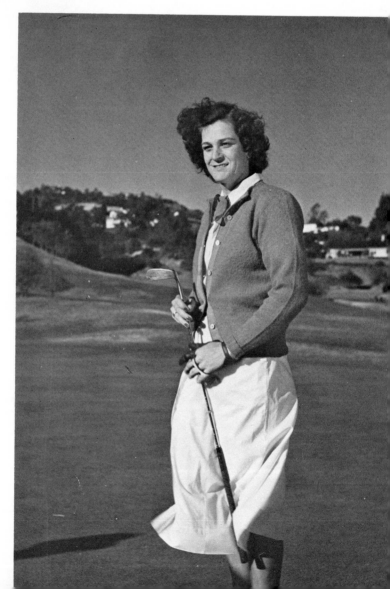

indicated that national opinion had flipped about, with 60 percent in favor of sending help, 40 percent opposed. War was almost at hand, and yet the bitter statistics of the Depression still prevailed: nine million Americans were unemployed in 1940 – eleven years after the Crash. It is interesting to note that while George Zaharias was making well over $100,000 a year on his wrestling promotions, more than half the families in America were existing on an annual income of $1,500. The Zahariases were rich by any standard of the day.

Babe's name appeared rarely in the sports pages in 1941, her eclipse was almost complete. As it turned out, it did not matter much that her golf career was in limbo: once war was declared after the Pearl Harbor attack on December 7, 1941, most formal sports programs in the United States were either canceled outright or severely curtailed. The Japanese attack had created waves of panic and frenzied patriotism everywhere in the U.S., but particularly in California. There were blackouts constantly and endless false reports of oncoming waves of "Nip" bombers or sightings of Admiral Tojo's fleet off Catalina Island. Early in 1942, George decided that he simply had to enlist; he wanted to teach the boys "unarmed defense" based on the wrestling holds he knew. He tried every branch of the services, but was rejected as unfit by all because of varicose veins. Had he been able to enlist, Babe planned to apply for a commission in the Women's Army Corps.

A certified 4-F, George arranged U.S.O. wrestling tours to military installations. Babe performed in a series of golf exhibitions to help sell defense bonds. She performed with Hollywood celebrities, including Johnny Weissmuller, Mickey Rooney, Bob Hope and Bing Crosby. Her ad lib gag routines with Hope and Crosby were practically the sporting hit of the war. She also did defense bond exhibitions (more playing and less talking) with golf stars such as Ben Hogan, Byron Nelson, Sam Snead and chubby young Patty Berg (then twenty-three).

Babe had polished up a sharp little show-biz golf routine with Gene Sarazen, which she used to great advantage. She would pile on her thickest honey-pie East Texas drawl and call out to the galleries: "Heah, you-all! You-all come closah nahow, 'cuz you-all've heerda Waltah Hagen and you-all heerda Bobbuh Jeeones, but today, folks, you-all ah lookin' at th' veruh best of 'em all – yoahs truleh, li'l ol' Babe Didrikson!" Then she would tee up to five balls and rapidly hit one after another until the fifth ball was soaring into the air from the tee before the first had hit the ground. After that, she would stack up two balls and hit one down the fairway, while the other popped up to drop into her pocket. And finally she would lay down a row of club shafts on a green, and putt a ball so it leaped – magically – over each club and rolled into the hole. Babe's attitude on the golf course was airy and lighthearted, a refreshing antithesis to the grim chess-match concentration many other players affected. She said, "I just love a gallery. It bothers some athletes to have people always crowding around them. I wouldn't feel right if the people weren't there. Even in a tournament, I like to kid around with the gallery."

On January 21, 1943, Babe emerged from her hiatus repurified – an amateur in good standing with the U.S.G.A. She celebrated her return within days by playing a thirty-six hole charity match against Clara Callender, the California women's champion. Babe was fantastic, shooting a 70 and a 67, which broke the women's record at the Desert Golf Club in Palm Springs. A week later, Babe beat Mrs. Callender for the midwinter championship at the Los Angeles Country Club. There was not that much left to compete in; the war had caused cancellation of nearly all major tournaments for the duration. It was difficult for anyone to travel – the trains were filled with troops; there was strict gasoline rationing. Those airlines that flew had most of their space reserved for Washington VIPs and military brass. Not until the summer of 1944 did Babe play in a major tournament. She managed to get to Indianapolis for the Western Open. She won easily. It was her first significant victory as an amateur. Home in Los Angeles again, she won a few California tournaments and played social golf with such diverse celebrities as Joe Louis and General Omar Bradley. In June 1945, she again made her way to Indianapolis for another Western Open. After victories in 1940 and 1944, she was trying to win her third championship there, something no one had done before.

Babe won her first match, then George phoned to tell Babe that her beloved mama had suffered a heart attack in Los Angeles. She was in critical condition, recovery was unlikely. Babe said she would return immediately, but George told her: "No, your mama wants you to finish the tournament." As it turned out, there was no choice: Babe could not get a seat on any plane or train out of Indianapolis. She played her quarterfinals match and won. The next day she played her semifinal match and won. That night, her sister Esther phoned to say that Mama had died. Now Babe was frantic to return, but her sister said, "No, you go ahead and win the tournament; that's the way Mama would want it."

Babe tried desperately to get transportation home but there was none. The night before the finals, she phoned Peggy Kirk Bell, who had met Babe for the first time only a few days earlier. Peggy recalled, "Babe asked me to have dinner with her, she asked me and my friend Marge Row to her apartment. We knew her mother had died and we all expected her to default. We didn't know what to expect that night. Babe just sat there and played her harmonica. She played for hours. I didn't think we'd ever eat. She didn't speak, she just kept playing the harmonica. I guess it was her way to overcome sadness. The next day she went out and beat Dorothy Germain and took the championship. When Babe first came out on the amateur circuit, lots of people didn't want her to win because they didn't think she should have been allowed to become an amateur. They always rooted for the young girls to beat her, but that day everyone was pulling for the old Babe to win because of her mother's death."

Babe shot a scorching 72 in the morning round against Miss Germain, then coasted through the second round to win the match four and two. She made some of her shots with tears in her eyes. At five the next morning, Babe wangled a seat on a plane. She was bumped in Kansas City for some brass with higher priority. She waited twelve hours for another plane, was bumped again in Albuquerque, waited more hours for another flight, was bumped once more in Phoenix, waited again and finally arrived in Los Angeles for her mother's funeral two full days after she left Indianapolis. It happened to fall on June 26, 1945, Babe's thirty-fourth birthday.

The war was over that August and now Babe began playing golf in earnest. The old major tournaments were gradually being revived. In the fall of 1945, she won the Texas Women's Open. Then she beat Betty Jameson in a series of matches that drew a lot of attention. She was her usual radiant cocksure self, her game was brilliant. In November 1945 she phoned Peggy Kirk Bell; it was the first time they had any contact since the strange evening in Indianapolis. "Suddenly, there she was on the telephone and I thought, wow, why is she calling me?" said Peggy. "Well, she wanted to know if I was going down to Florida and if I would be her partner in the Hollywood four-ball tournament. What she actually said was, 'I need a partner for that four-ball and you might as well win a tournament.' Well, I was thrilled. Then when I arrived in Florida I got very nervous about playing with her. She asked why. I told her that if we lost it would be my fault. She stared at me and said, 'Look, Peggy, I can beat any two of 'em. I'll let you know if I need you.' She won everything in sight.

Babe was so confident, she was hard to compete against. But she didn't purposely psych people out. I once took a seven on a first hole and Babe came over to me and said, 'Now Peggy, why don't you see if you can just par from here on in.' It boosted me up and I shot a seventy-four and took second place. She used to kid me about practicing all the time. She'd go in the bar and have a drink while I went out and practiced. She'd say, 'I can lie in bed and fix my golf swing.' She could visualize it. She had put in all those years of practicing, but when I got to know her in nineteen forty-five, she didn't practice much anymore. It's funny, I used to think she was holding back on me, that she had some secret about her game she wouldn't tell. But I really don't think Babe knew that much about teaching people, she played the game by feel and strength. She was a natural and she couldn't pass that on.

"By the time I met Babe, she was not tough or manly. Sometimes she overdressed a little – she'd wear frilly blouses that didn't look right. She was best in tailored things. She could go anywhere. Golf was a more social sport then than now and it lifted Babe up. It made her appreciate the good things in life. She was so proud of being a golfer. She never even talked about the Olympics or all her other sports."

After the 1945 season, the Associated Press voted her the outstanding woman athlete for the year, and in 1946 tournament golf returned to its full prewar schedule. The country was relieved, relaxed, beginning to anticipate enormous prosperity and leisure after the sacrifice and tensions of the war. Sport was in fantastic ascendancy and Babe became one of the leading figures – again. As an amateur, Babe dominated women's golf as no one ever has; she was its unbeatable queen.

In the summer of 1946 she began a string of consecutive victories never approached by man or woman. For more than a year Babe

Didrikson Zaharias did not lose a match: she won *seventeen* straight tournaments. The closest anyone has come to this record was Byron Nelson with eleven straight in 1945. Included in Babe's grand chain was the National Woman's Amateur (the premier American title), which she won by an unbelievable score of eleven up with *nine* holes to play. She won the Helen Doherty Women's Amateur by twelve strokes up with *ten* holes to play, the Broadmoor Match Play by ten and nine, and the Women's Titleholder in Augusta, Georgia – a mini-Masters for women – where she overcame a *ten-stroke* deficit to win with a medal score of 304, five strokes ahead of the field. For the record: she also won the Texas Open, the All-American at Tam O'Shanter, a second Broadmoor Invitational, the Tampa Open, the Palm Beach Women's Amateur, South Atlantic, Florida East Coast, North & South, the Hollywood Four-Ball, the Florida Mixed Two-Ball, the Celebrities Championship and – the most sparkling gem in the necklace – the British Women's Amateur.

This noble old competition was known officially as "The Ladies Amateur Golf Championship Tournament, Under the Management of the Ladies Golf Union." No American had won since the tournament began in 1893, although Glenna Collett Vare had gone to the finals a couple of times, only to lose to the magnificent Joyce Wethered. In 1947 the Ladies Amateur was to be held in June at Gullane, Scotland. At this point, Babe's streak had reached fifteen consecutive tournaments and had been heavily publicized in American and British newspapers. It was Babe's first trip to Europe, but she could scarcely have been more at home. In the medieval village of Gullane, she stayed in the North Berwick Inn, a craggy old institution that had been in business for hundreds of years. Her fame had preceded her: she sat down for breakfast on her first morning there and said apologetically that she'd like bacon or ham, eggs, fried potatoes, toast and coffee for breakfast – "but I don't suppose I can get that here, can I?" (postwar food rationing was still very strict in Great Britain then). The man who waited on her replied cheerily, "Mrs. Zaharias, we have all of that. The manager wanted to have the things you're used to eating and he has been keeping some chickens just for you and he went to an American boat and got enough bacon and ham for your whole stay here."

She took to walking the cobbled streets of the town from the inn to the golf course, and she was surprised to find that more people knew her by sight in Gullane than might have in the South End of Beaumont. They constantly called out greetings to her. She nodded and shouted Texas howdies to Scots farmers across ancient stone fences and she often accepted on-the-spot invitations to tea from housewives who lived in houses that were hundreds of years old. People at first called her "Mrs. Zaharias" but she asked the local newspaper to print a story asking them to please call her "Babe." This was done.

Gullane was a rough and lovely seaside course, lashed by fierce winds and inhabited by wandering flocks of sheep. When Babe played her practice rounds, the club arranged for a man in a white coat to accompany her for the singular purpose of cleaning the greens of sheep droppings before she putted. That section of Scotland was so far north that it was light at that time of year until far into the night, and Babe often practiced after dinner. The management of the North Berwick Inn thoughtfully provided blackout curtains for the windows of her room so she could sleep despite the long nighttime hours of semi-daylight. Along one fairway there was a street lined with large old houses, and whenever Babe practiced, the windows and the front stoops of those houses were filled with curious Scots watching the famous American play their beloved game. Sometimes Babe would perform her trick shots for her fans in the houses.

The weather turned raw and wet soon after she arrived and the newspapers printed a story saying that Mrs. Zaharias had not brought proper attire for such cold days. Immediately, her hotel room was flooded with bundles containing heavy clothing; eventually so many packages arrived that they had to pile them in the lobby and hallways. From these "Bundles for Babe" she chose a World War II siren suit and a pair of baggy light blue corduroy slacks to wear against the inclement weather; the rest were returned or sent to camps for displaced persons. When the tournament began, Babe wore the corduroys almost every day and all of Scotland came to refer to them familiarly as "Babe's slocks." She continued her flamboyant ways even during serious tournament play. Once a dignified old man watched in awe as she smashed a drive close to three hundred yards. When he asked her how she could manage such distance, Babe grinned and shocked him with her best-known crack, "I just take off my girdle and beat the ball, sir!" Once after a winning round, she did a loose-jointed Texas style highland fling on the clubhouse lawn – barefoot and wearing a kilt.

Not everyone appreciated her antics, of course. One day three elderly ladies in proper tweeds and woolen stockings approached Mrs. A. M. Holm, one of England's fine golfers and a quarterfinalist that year, and declared that they felt Mrs. Zaharias to be boastful, immodest, tasteless and altogether lacking in refinement. Mrs. Holm retorted coldly, "You are speaking of the finest woman golfer that has ever been seen here."

Large galleries followed her and murmured politely after every shot. This aura of quiet was a traditional Scottish courtesy intended to allow players to concentrate and perform in an environment approaching the splendid isolation of a hospital zone. They refrained from applause at spectacular shots. This troubled Babe, for she had long grown accustomed to clowning and chattering with relatively raucous American crowds. Despite the pervasive quiet, she won her first match easily, then went on to win her second match on the sixteenth hole. Babe decided to finish the round by playing the two remaining by-holes. On the seventeenth tee, she did one of her trick shots: she teed up a ball and slily stood a kitchen match behind it so the head was flush against the ball. When she hit it, the match exploded with an astonishingly loud report – "Like a small cannon," Babe recalled. The gallery started in surprise, then began to laugh, then watched in wonder as the drive flew nearly three hundred yards down the fairway; the crowd began to cheer, then burst into roaring applause. The ball landed in a trap just off the green and from there Babe did another of her tricks. She set a second ball atop the one in the sand, swung a chipping iron gently: the top ball flew up and landed in her pocket, the other one skittered nicely across the green – and dropped into the hole! This was the stuff of legend, of fantasy. The crowd roared, hooted, laughed aloud like children. Finally, on the eighteenth green, with the clubhouse porch overflowing with people, Babe strode up to her ball, addressed it, then turned around, bent over and – backwards between her legs – putted it into the hole. The delighted bellow that rose could be heard in the farthest corner of the course. Afterward she was engulfed in a throng of adoring, grinning Scotsmen and she signed autographs for nearly an hour by the eighteenth green.

The next day a sign saying "Please Do Not Play The By-Holes" was posted in the clubhouse, but Babe had delighted everyone with her unorthodox foolishness, and her galleries grew larger and noisier every day. In the semifinals, she played one of Britain's best, Jean Donald. The gallery was estimated at close to eight thousand people – a larger crowd than had watched the British men's amateur tournament at Carnoustie two weeks earlier. As with all of the early matches, this one with Mrs. Donald was over only eighteen holes; Babe won *seven* up with five holes to go, an overwhelmingly lopsided score in such a short match.

The morning of the final – a thirty-six hole match against Jacqueline Gordon – the weather was warm and sunny for the first time since the tournament began. Babe wore a light sweater and skirt and left her siren suit and corduroy slacks at the North Berwick Inn. Midway through the first eighteen holes the sky grew dark, the wind picked up and Babe began to shiver. She had brought only a light outer sweater with her and it was not enough to ward off the chill. At lunch the match stood even. As Babe headed for the clubhouse several anxious Scotsmen said to her, "Babe, go get your *slocks* on. Get your slocks on." She hurried back to the Inn to change. On the way, she wanted to get her golf shoes adjusted slightly, but when she stopped at the shoemaker's shop a sign in the window said, "Sorry. Closed. Gone to see Babe." Someone had to summon the cobbler from the golf course to do the work.

When Babe returned for the afternoon round, she was wearing her "lucky slocks." She parred the first hole and went one hole up on Miss Gordon. She eagled the par-five second hole, to go two up. She parred the third to go three up. She kept the pressure on Miss Gordon and was five holes up going into the last nine. Babe then lost a hole, but it was the only one of the entire afternoon. She won the British Ladies' championship on the thirty-second hole where she went five up with four holes to play. The gallery burst into an ovation that lasted for several minutes. Babe was as elated as a child at a birthday party. When photographers asked her to come around to the front of the clubhouse for pictures, she broke into a sprint and hurdled a small brick wall to get there. She danced a little Highland Fling, sang a

Scottish ditty and joyously told everyone that she had not put on her "slocks" for luck but for warmth.

Her joie de vivre and her booming power game had caught the imagination of all Britain. The Manchester *Guardian* was ecstatic about her victory:

Surely no woman golfer has accomplished in a championship what Mrs. Zaharias has achieved in this one. She has never had to go beyond the 16th green and she has lost only four holes in six rounds and her score for the holes she has played yesterday and today approximate to an average of fours over a course that measures 6600 yards. She has combined in a remarkable way immense length with accuracy, reaching with a number-five iron holes at which others are content to be short with a wood. She is a crushing and heart-breaking opponent.

Babe played several of Scotland's celebrated old courses, just for fun, then headed for America – a heroine on two continents. When her train left Edinburgh for London, hundreds crowded together on the platform to sing "Auld Lang Syne." She sailed for home on the *Queen Mary,* and when the great liner was still three hours out of New York Harbor, a tugboat steamed up alongside. It was loaded to overflowing with reporters, photographers, newsreel cameramen – seventy-one of them. In the midst of the crowd stood George, a beaming behemoth in a massive wrinkled white shirt. When the tugboat came alongside, he led the crowd up a rope ladder onto the main deck. Babe and George hugged, kissed and then the press asked Babe to put on a tartan cap and kilt. She did. So did George. They danced, they kissed, they laughed for the cameras. She was the queen of her game. The Zahariases stayed in New York only briefly. Among Babe's visitors was Fred Corcoran, the quick-witted director of the Men's Professional

Golf, Association and one of the best sports agents in the business. Corcoran told Babe that he would like to represent her if she ever turned professional again. She declared that was the furthest thing from her mind – and perhaps it was then. She and George took an airliner to Denver where they now lived. George hated to fly (his vast size made him anxious that any plane he was on might be dangerously overloaded), but they had to hurry home because the city of Denver had arranged a massive reception. There was a parade, which included several floats fixed to represent different sports Babe had played – basketball, baseball, hurdling, etc. She rode on the last float herself, grinning, waving, engulfed in a sea of roses. At the city hall she was given a two-hundred-and-fifty-pound key to the city, which even George could barely lift. About fifty thousand people came to her parade and it was a grand public celebration such as she hadn't experienced since her jubilant return to Dallas after the Olympics.

Babe relaxed for a couple of weeks, then played in the Broadmoor Tournament at Colorado Springs in mid-July. She won. It was her seventeenth straight victory. By now, however, there was a steady incoming flood of offers to turn professional. George had been spending as much as $15,000 a year to keep her on the amateur circuit. He could well afford it, but it seemed the time had come to cash in. The offer that finally convinced her came from a movie company; she would be paid $300,000 to make ten short films on golf. Ironically the deal fell flat. Nevertheless, on the strength of it, Babe and George drove back to New York, contacted the doughty Fred Corcoran, and on August 14, 1947, Babe turned professional once more, with Corcoran as her manager. Corcoran was seventy years old in 1975, a gray-haired, lively fellow with sparkling blue eyes, a cheery round face and a slight tangy Boston accent. He has been known for years as Mr. Golf; his career effectively began when he was a caddy for Francis Ouimet in 1914, and he later became director of the men's professional circuit in 1936, a noted golf historian and agent for some of the best in the game, including Sam Snead, Tony Lema, and Ken Venturi. Fred Corcoran recalled his dealings with Babe: "When she signed, I had never met George. They came up to my office in New York and I asked George what kind of contract he wanted for her. He told me, 'You and Babe work everything out.' We did, and later we had a press conference at Toots Shor's. At the time, I was also handling Ted Williams, Stan Musial and Snead. They were great guys, but when it came to getting headlines, Babe had them all beat. She had a fantastic feel for publicity. At the press conference she told why she was turning pro, then the thing started to drag a little, so she opened it up for questions. A guy asked her what her plans were – where was she going to play? 'Well,' she said, 'I'm going to enter the U.S. Open Championship – for *men.*' I didn't know she was going to say this. I don't think she did when she got up there. There was this stunned silence, mouths dropped and then the press – en masse – made a dash for the phones. At the time, there was no rule against women entering the men's Open but the very next day the U.S.G.A. put in a new rule forbidding it. However, Babe had gotten her headlines. She had upstaged them all."

When Babe and Fred signed their contract, she had said, "Okay, I'll get the charity matches, you get the ones for dough." Immediately Corcoran had her performing in ball parks all over the country – Yankee Stadium, Detroit, Chicago. She was paid $500 a night for a little act that included playing third base during batting practice, taking a few cuts at the plate and hitting golf shots into the outfield. Once at Yankee Stadium a ground ball got past her; she whooped in anger, ripped her skirt up the side and dug in by the bag, scooping up grounder after grounder to prove her excellence as an infielder.

The crowd loved her in ballparks as much as they did on golf courses. Corcoran recalled: "Once in Detroit, Billy Evans, the owner, kept saying he thought the price was four hundred and fifty dollars instead of five hundred. The stadium was sold out because Detroit was playing the Red Sox and Ted Williams was a big draw. Well, we bickered back and forth, finally he agreed. Just before the game it started to rain. The umpire put off the start and Babe went out and entertained for an hour in the rain. The crowd stayed put and they gave her a standing ovation. The game ended up being cancelled, but Babe had given the fans their money's worth. They used to love having her come into restaurants, too. They'd give her these huge steaks. She'd break up the whole place with gags and she'd play her harmonica. She was always entertaining people."

Babe's victory string was still intact at the point she turned professional. Then in October, she returned to Fort Worth for the Texas Open. She got to the quarterfinals on October 9, 1947, and teed off against a young amateur named Betty Mims White. Babe's game was flat and she was three down to Miss White after fifteen holes. She rallied and won the sixteenth and the seventeenth holes to be just one down with one hole to play. Babe birdied the last hole, then stood by as Betty Mims White lined up a six-foot putt for a birdie. She sank it and that cut Babe's string at seventeen. Betty Mims White was never heard from again. Babe was undaunted. She charged on to win her next tournament, something called the Hardscrabble Women's Open in Little Rock, Arkansas. She was spectacular: she had a seventy-two hole score of 293, an average of 73-plus per round which was an all time tournament record for women.

Her game had never been better, and once more in 1947 she was named Woman Athlete of the Year. Now the problem was essentially the same as it had been before: there simply weren't that many tournaments for women pros – a few more than in the 1930s but not many, and the money was a pittance. In 1948, Babe was the leading tournament money-winner: she won exactly $3,400. Of course this was only the tiniest fraction of her total income. Corcoran said: "Babe was getting six hundred dollars for a golf exhibition when men like Ben Hogan and Sam Snead were only getting five hundred. She was making all kinds of personal appearances and she had an eight-thousand-dollar-a-year contract with Wilson – for life."

With everything added together, she made over $100,000. That was about the same as Ted Williams. But – as always – Babe craved competition. Also, she liked tournaments because they generated more publicity, which generated more money. She and Corcoran decided to enlarge the women's pro golf tour. "We needed money, of course," said Corcoran. "L. B. Icely, the president of Wilson, thought he saw some kind of a future in women's golf and he was willing to put up the money. There had been something called the Women's Professional Golf Association earlier. I called Hope Seignious, who was the head of it; she refused to sell us the charter. Well, okay, we thought, in England they call them 'ladies' and in a way it sounded classier than 'women.' We decided to call our tour the 'Ladies' Professional Golf Association.' "

And so the L.P.G.A. was born and women's golf was never the same again.

Chapter
13

The charter membership of the Ladies Professional Golf Association numbered six. They were Babe Didrikson Zaharias, Patty Berg, Helen Dettweiler, Betty Jameson, Betty Hicks and Bea Gottlieb. This was a select but relatively deprived little group. None was in any way prospering from the sport, except for Babe and Patty Berg. Patty had turned professional in 1940 when she was twenty-two and, like Babe, had a contract with L. B. Icely's Wilson Company. In January 1948, Babe, Patty, George and Fred Corcoran got together at the Venetian Hotel in Miami and in a couple of afternoons laid out the new L.P.G.A. Patty volunteered to be president that first year. L. B. Icely put up the prize money – $15,000.

And that was all there was in 1949 – $15,000 over nine tournaments. Babe Zaharias ended up as the leading money-winner with a mere $4,300. Despite its puny beginning, it was obvious that the L.P.G.A. was an excellent idea whose time had come: it grew with astounding rapidity, attracting dozens of new members and thousands of new dollars in the first year. In 1950 Babe was the leading winner with $13,450 and in 1951 she won $15,087 – more than they had for the whole tour two years before. In the first five years, the total L.P.G.A. prize money multiplied fifteenfold – to $225,000.

As the money poured in and more women began competing, rivalries were born. Babe's most intense rival was Louise Suggs, a chunky brunette from Atlanta. Louise was stoic, very serious, a colorless person who was almost completely humorless. She was, however, a superb golfer and her record was almost as good as Babe's. Because of her withdrawn personality, Louise never got the adoring press coverage that Babe did. Suggs won the British Women's Amateur in 1948, the year after Babe, and the feat received about half the coverage Babe's victory had, and there was certainly no tugboat full of reporters to greet Louise when she returned. Even when she defeated Babe, the headlines as often as not said BABE LOSES rather than LOUISE WINS. These things grated on her, naturally. She also disapproved of Babe's loud, flamboyant behavior; she believed that golf should be a dignified game and that Babe's quips and tricks on the course were disgraceful.

Once Louise was silently frowning over a crucial putt on the eighteenth green of a tournament. The gallery was hushed, Louise lined it up, poised to hit it and at the instant she took her putter back to strike the ball Babe and Betty Dodd suddenly cut loose on the clubhouse porch with a hillbilly song, Babe tootling her harmonica and Betty twanging her guitar. Louise jerked, hit the ball, missed the putt. She was enraged and stalked off the course. Babe and Betty swore it was an accident, that they hadn't known she was on the green. Louise refused to talk to either of them for days, convinced they had done it purposely to ruin her shot.

Fred Corcoran recalled: "Babe could do anything – play the mouth organ, dance, kid around with the press. Louise was always in her shadow. I'd set up a tournament and try to promote them with flashy little gimmicks. You know, I'd bring Humphrey Bogart out to kiss the winner of the tournament, things like that. Babe loved it, but

Suggs? Once she won, and instead of standing there to be kissed, she screamed and ran into the locker room."

Not everyone felt Louise's dislike for Babe was entirely misplaced. Betsy Rawls, who was installed in the Women's Golf Hall of Fame in 1960, recalled: "Louise was the frankest and most outspoken player on the tour. I think Babe felt threatened by Suggs. Louise played with dignity and by the rules. The two of them were playing at the Tam once and Babe dropped her ball halfway across the fairway. They came in at the end of the round and Suggs wouldn't sign her card. One of the sponsors said, 'Here, I'll sign it.' But Suggs lost all respect for Babe after that." Justified or not, Louise's dislike for Babe was a consuming emotion. Even when Babe was near the end of her life at a Galveston hospital in 1956, she refused to relent. Peggy Kirk Bell recalled: "I phoned Louise and told her Babe was dying and said, 'You know she is not going to be here for her next birthday.' I told her Babe's birthday was coming up and we thought it would be great if the L.P.G.A. members all sent her flowers. George even said he would pay for them if everyone would remember Babe on her birthday. Suggs told me she would and promised Betty Dodd that she would. I talked to Babe on the night of her birthday and she said what a great party she had in the hospital and how everyone sent her flowers except Suggs. I told Babe there must be some mistake, that I was sure Louise had sent some. No, Babe said, she didn't. Babe was really hurt, she wanted people to like her, she really cared about it. Well, I called Suggs and said, 'You did send flowers, didn't you, Louise?' 'No, I didn't,' she said. 'I decided I'm not going to be a hypocrite about this thing.' Oh, I could have crucified her for that. Had I known, I would have sent some and signed her name."

Nevertheless, even Betty Dodd felt Suggs might have been justified in her dislike for Babe. "Babe played with her like a cat plays with a mouse," said Betty. "Suggs had a better record than Babe and she felt – rightly so – that she did not get the credit she deserved. I liked Louise. She was nice to me and she didn't hold it against me that I was Babe's friend. I was furious when she wouldn't send flowers to Babe. Babe was sick, all her defenses were on the floor. Babe had written Louise two or three letters trying to call off the vendetta. I knew Babe did this because I read the letters. Babe was in tears that Louise hadn't sent flowers and when I got off the phone I tore into Louise. She was standing with this group of people and I shouted at her – 'How could you be so cruel!' My voice got louder and louder and she started to cry and finally walked out. After this blowup she and I were still good friends. I really couldn't hold it against Louise because I knew what Babe had done to her."

Babe was an overpowering, often an overbearing force on the tour, and many women resented her. Betsy Rawls said, "She really was a rather crude person. She added a lot of color to the tour at the time when it was needed, but she did not add any dignity to the game. She was the L.P.G.A.'s first big drawing card and she was not above using this as leverage to get her way. If it started to rain and she was playing badly, she'd get them to call the round off. She didn't always play by the rules. I don't think she cheated, but she did bend the rules. Above all, she wanted to win and she would sacrifice other things to win. She could intimidate sponsors into letting her have her way. She couldn't get away with that today, but that's the way she had grown up. She didn't have any money and she would use any device to win. She could be very ungracious when she lost, and when things didn't go her way, she could be mean. When things went her way, she was fun and pleasant to be with."

Babe was in the habit of demanding appearance money for most tournaments and most sponsors were willing to give it to her since she attracted hundreds of people who would not buy a ticket to a tournament without her. George May, who ran the All-American tournaments at his Tam O'Shanter club in Niles, Illinois, used to create a weak subterfuge about the appearance payment by telling Babe: "I'll give you an extra thousand dollars if you break eighty." But other players bitterly resented this practice and, once, Betty Hicks wrote an article criticizing Babe publicly. Babe was then president of the L.P.G.A. and she called a meeting of the membership, sat them all down and declared, "Let me tell you girls something: you know when there's a star, like in show business, the star has her name in lights on the marquee! Right? And the star gets the money because the people come to see the star, right? Well, *I'm* the star and all of you are in the chorus. *I* get the money and if it weren't for me, half of our tournaments wouldn't even be." The assembly was stunned. Peggy Kirk Bell recalled: "Everyone was there – Berg, Suggs, *everyone*. Well, Babe was right, she was the star, but I told her afterward, 'Babe, you shouldn't have said it. I would have said it for you.' But Babe didn't work that way. She was totally honest and she said what she thought."

However blunt and outspoken she may have been there was no question that Babe Zaharias was the most important woman in the L.P.G.A. She was its fulcrum, its energy source, its creative genius. Patty Berg said, "Babe changed the game of golf for women – not only by bringing along the L.P.G.A., but by her kind of golf. She came along with that great power game and it led to lower scores and more excitement. She even changed the swing. It used to be built on the Scottish method and we hit waist high, more flat. Babe would swing high and hard. And she brought all that humor and showmanship to the game. She humanized it. She was the happiest girl you ever saw, like a kid. Our sport grew because of Babe, because she had so much flair and color. She and I were in competition with each other but she was a great friend of mine. Sometimes I find myself leaning back in a chair thinking about Babe, and I have to smile – with Babe there was never a dull moment. Her tremendous enthusiasm for golf and life was contagious – even the galleries felt good when Babe was around."

Despite her dominance and her influence on the game, Babe's swing never did groove into the fluid sweet arc that Sam Snead or Mickey Wright developed. There were flaws that got her in trouble. Her grip was a problem for years – too much fist, not enough fingers as Stan Kertes had long ago diagnosed. Although she was celebrated for her immense power – booming long drives, which many men could not match (she once hit a ball four hundred and nine yards) – her tee shots were the most troublesome element of her game because they were sometimes so wild. Experts agree that Britain's Joyce Wethered was a better golfer and some say that the American Mickey Wright is, too.

Although many of her fans overlooked it in favor of her booming drives, Babe did have a sharp, subtle short game. Alice Bauer, who began playing the L.P.G.A. tour in 1949, said: "I'm always getting scared and I never know whether the ball is going right or left, but Babe could tell you what blade of grass it would land on." As for her putting, Patty Berg said, "She was just great. From four feet, she never missed, and that is unusual for a long hitter." Often golfers were struck with the look of her hands – graceful, tapered fingers and a gentle light touch that was sheer magic with a golf club. She possessed the gliding buoyance of a born athlete, a perfectly controlled coordination when she addressed the ball, a feeling she described as "standing on eggs." Betsy Rawls summarized Babe's game this way: "She was the most physically talented woman I have ever seen and if she had started golf at an earlier age she would have been sensational. But she never developed to her full potential. She was strongest around the greens, she had that very soft touch, but she often mis-hit her drives and she did not have a classic swing. She was so strong that she didn't have to develop her swing and there were flaws in it. She had moments of greatness when she put it all together, but she had trouble being consistent because of her faulty swing. She was often in trouble but she was a great scrambler."

She was also a relentless competitor, never content to give any quarter to anyone – not even her closest friends. She once lent Betty Dodd a driver and another time let Peggy Kirk Bell borrow an eleven-iron. Both immediately used the new clubs with excellent results. In both cases, Babe said after a few holes, "I believe I'll take that club back now," and she did. She would try to outwit, one-up and outdo her opponents in any way she could. She would hit a five-iron, then quickly stuff it back into the bag and declare that it was a seven. She would stride into a locker room before a tournament and cry out, "Okay, Babe's here! Now who's gonna finish second?" She would exaggerate her practice score to impress her opponents. Peggy Kirk Bell recalled, "We were playing a tournament in Denver and Babe shot an eighty in a practice round. The press came up and asked her score, 'Oh, about a seventy, I guess,' she said. I was horrified and I said, 'But, Babe, you shot an eighty.' She said, 'Well, I could have had a seventy if I tried.' "

She constantly played to the galleries, of course. She would wink and say to them as she addressed the ball, "Okay, folks, now you are about to see a shot you have never seen before." Sometimes when she was in deep trouble and required an impossible shot to get out, she would step back from the ball and give the crowd a guided tour of precisely where she meant for the coming shot to go: "I'll hit it toward that tree branch there, then it'll angle to the left a little, then turn slightly right to go through that itty-bitty opening, then it'll climb and climb and land on the green. You just watch." When the shot was done, every person in the gallery would swear the ball had done all those things.

She was almost always completely at ease, no matter how intense the pressure. She rarely displayed her temper during a tournament. But if she hit a poor shot, she tended to blame some outside cause rather than herself.

Betty Dodd said, "She always had an excuse – that son of a bitching cameraman clicked his shutter just when I was putting or something like that. She could, at times, have a foul mouth if she was really angry. She was poker-faced in tournaments, though. I never saw her throw a club or anything like that, not in a tournament. But she could not stand to lose – anything. We were out once in a foursome in Tampa, just playing for a dollar Nassau. Babe missed several putts. She just stopped, stood there and all of a sudden she snapped the putter over her knee like a toothpick. Then she hauled off and threw the pieces into the woods. She scared the rest of us to death. We didn't say one word the rest of the way in."

In 1950, Fred Corcoran arranged a tour of England for the six best players in the L.P.G.A. Babe was number one, the others were Peggy Kirk Bell, Patty Berg, Betsy Rawls, Betty Jameson and Betty MacKinnon. Predictably enough they were scheduled to play a series of matches against Britain's best women, but Corcoran had also arranged an unprecedented match to be played against any men's team the English cared to assemble. It was public-relations gimmickry of sorts, but the women were deadly serious about this – particularly Babe. Ultimately it was arranged for the women to play members of the Walker Cup team, essentially the cream of male amateur golfers in

England. Babe was to play Leonard Crawley, former team captain; Crawley had told Corcoran that he was particularly keen to play "that Babe person." When they met at the first tee Crawley pointed up toward the women's tee and said, "Now, Mildred you go up there and hit." Babe replied, "Hell, no, I'm goin' to stay back here and hit with you, son." Then she added, "Leonard, I'd like to make you a bet. If I beat you, I want you to shave off that big ol' mustache, is that a deal?" Crawley had a lush handlebar mustache; Babe had purposely spoken loud enough so all of the reporters following the match overheard. Babe proceeded to shoot a smashing 74, giving Leonard Crawley a severe trouncing. He walked directly off the eighteenth green, got in his car and drove away without saying a word. The press ribbed him sharply for several days and several sportswriters wrote thoughtful columns about how Leonard Crawley would look clean-shaven. The other five women also won their matches that day for a 6–0 score over the Walker Cuppers, and even though most of the losing Britons were better sportsmen than Leonard Crawley, it was a day of dark humiliation for England.

During another competition, Babe and Patty Berg were teamed in a best-ball match against two Walker Cuppers named Davenport and Beck. Patty recalled Babe's intense competitive nature that day: "We were one down on the seventeenth hole and Babe drove one way out into the heather. She said, 'Don't worry, Patty, we're going to pull this thing out. We'll tie this hole and eagle the next one. All you have to do now is get this on the green.' I say, 'Fine, fine, Babe, but I've got to *find* the ball first.' Finally I did find it and I did hit it on the green. Now Babe is determined to putt first. She keeps saying to me, 'Look when I sink this putt, they'll tighten up and they'll blow it.' Well, Davenport is convinced that his ball is out and he has the right to putt first. Babe is beside herself over this. It is counter to her strategy. Davenport is lining up the putt and he is standing over it all ready for his backswing and all of a sudden Babe shrieks, 'TIME OUT!' We all look at her. *'Time out?'* It is the first and last time I'd ever heard this expression on a golf course, but Babe was determined to stop him. Everyone was horrified. A distinguished gentleman comes out on the green and talks very quietly to Babe. She gestures like mad and tries to convince him that she should putt first. He stares at her and then he says, very stiffly, no, Davenport will putt first. Davenport sinks his, Babe sinks ours and we move to the eighteenth tee, still one stroke down to them. Now Babe hits the longest drive I have ever seen. We get an eagle, we take the hole and we tie them for the match. She picked me up and carried me right off the green."

Babe was a constant prankster on the tour who kept everyone on edge or in laughter at her tricks. She would put a hair brush in her roommate's bed, then shriek with laughter at the screams. She would disguise her voice on the phone, putting on outlandish German accents or pretending to be a tiny girl. Peggy Kirk Bell recalled: "I had a very aristocratic-type aunt and one day Babe was in her living room and she lifted up her leg onto a coffee table and said, 'Hey, Aunt Isabelle, isn't that the best-looking leg you ever did see?' My poor aunt just mumbled and looked away. The year I won the four-ball tournament with Babe, nineteen forty-five, I stayed with her on part of the tour. I didn't know her that well then and once we were staying at some people's home in Orlando. I got up and went to the bathroom and when I came back it looked like Babe was in bed. But she had stuffed pillows in it to look that way, she was really under my bed. Just when I was dropping off to sleep she grabbed my foot. I screeched and leaped a mile and she just laughed and laughed. Another time my bed kept moving, I couldn't figure it out. I'd just be off to sleep and I'd feel this jerk. Babe had tied a rope to the springs of my bed and she'd pull it from her bed and jar me. Life was never dull with Babe. She was just a great big overgrown kid who loved living. She loved every minute, more than anyone I've ever known."

Chapter 14

Healthy though the L.P.G.A. was, not even the most successful players could live in any high style on prize money alone. The most cash Babe ever won in a single tournament (not counting sub rosa appearance money) was $2,100. The most prize money she won in a year was $15,087. Everyone on the tour had to keep hustling up extra jobs, exhibitions, endorsements. Babe was better at this, too, than anyone on the tour.

At one point she was representing Grossinger's resort in the Catskill mountains on the tour, then she took a job as the resident professional at Chicago's Sky Crest Country Club. She was the first woman to hold such a position and she was paid $20,000 a year for it. It was very good money, but eventually Babe became restive, and in the summer of 1951 she wrote a letter to her friends the Bowens, saying:

We have been trying to get out of this job here in Chicago since the Jews came in. But guess we are going to have to fulfill our contract. George is bringing a fellow in from Denver to take over the pro shop for the rest of this season and also for next season. As there is no rest for him or me. As long as I am here they all want me for lessons. If I did give them they would have me out there all day long. Even if you charge them $50 per hour it doesn't make any difference. They pay and love it, but I'm not as hungry as I use to be. Rather play R. L. the rocks game for 25¢ and lose a couple of bucks which I don't pay anyway.

Ultimately, Babe was asked to leave the Sky Crest job because many of the members thought she was hustling them for extra money.

Babe was an inveterate freeloader, an eternal dealer and wheeler, always promoting something for nothing. Her homes were filled with appliances – electric saws, coffee makers, clock radios, sewing machines – that she or George had promoted. Babe demanded free hotel rooms, free meals, free gasoline, whenever she went to a tournament. She was blatant, unembarrassed about asking for what she wanted. Her favorite saying when she saw something she liked was, "Hey, I'm gonna *git* me one a those." As often as not she would simply walk into a store, tell the proprietor who she was and *ask* for what she wanted. Once when she discovered that a rich oil man in Oklahoma had given Byron Nelson a horse, she called the man, an old friend, and said, "Hey, I'd like a horse just like that one you gave Byron." The man gave her a similar horse which she kept for a long time but never did ride – even though she promoted a complete riding outfit, including jodhpurs and handsome leather boots to go with the horse.

Betty Dodd recalled one of Babe's more outrageous acts of freeloading: "One day we were in New York, just walking down the street, and Babe spotted a Rolex gold watch in a store window. She said, 'I've always wanted one of those watches.' I told her, 'Well if you want it so badly, why don't you go in and buy it?' She said, 'I ain't goin' to buy it! I'm gonna go *git* me one.' Well, she walks into a drugstore and looks up the phone number for Rolex. The next thing I know she is hailing a taxi and we go to the Rolex offices. She tells me, 'Now, you hush up.' We go up in an elevator and she walks up to this receptionist who was behind a window and says, 'I want to see the boss. I'm Babe Zaharias, tell him I'm here and tell him I want to see him.'

"I could have died, I was embarrassed to death. The secretary closes the panel, she looks at Babe as if she was nuts and then goes in this office door. Suddenly this man steps out and says I'm so-and-so, Babe, please come in. I told Babe, 'You go in, I'll stay here.' I wanted to crawl under the carpet. Well, Babe is in there with him for about thirty minutes. When they come out they are both smiling and laughing. He was the PR man for Rolex and he was thrilled to meet her. They set up a date to play golf the next day at Winged Foot and Rolex was going to have a luncheon for her. At the lunch Babe is given a gold Rolex. Then they gave *me* a gold Rolex. Then she got *another* one for George. In those days the watch was worth a thousand dollars. I was embarrassed to death, but she didn't think a thing of it."

Babe's endless desire to get things free might have been a throwback to her days of poverty, a compulsion to gather as much of value around her as she could since someday she might have nothing again. Or perhaps it was an extension of her competitive personality – a way of "winning" a contest by beating the system out of its material without paying.

In the early years of their marriage, George had masterminded most of the deals, but by 1953 Babe was as canny at picking up extra money as he. Betty Dodd recalled another trip to Manhattan. "We were going to be on an Ed Sullivan show – for the Cancer Society. Babe asked Sullivan, 'How much am I getting?' He told her fifteen hundred dollars. 'Well,' she said, 'I'm going to bring Betty Dodd, how much are you going to pay her?' He said three hundred dollars. After this show, she was asked to appear on "What's My Line?" and then more programs started to call her to make appearances. She always asked,

'How much are you going to pay me?' and before they could answer, she said, 'You pay me a thousand dollars and I'll be there.' Some of them hung up, but then they would call her back and agree to her terms. She arranged an exhibition match in Montreal and she got a thousand dollars for this, too. When we got back to New York, she phoned George and she was ecstatic. She said, 'Honey! I've made six thousand dollars in three weeks!' George was furious. He told her, 'You get home!' He knew he was losing control of her, that she didn't need him. She was really mad. She slammed down the phone and said, 'God damn him! If he thinks I'm going to go home so he can book me for three hundred dollars in some exhibition, he's crazy!' "

The Zaharias marriage had been troubled for several years. George, a man of gross appetite, weighed close to four hundred pounds. Their hotel rooms were often stocked like a delicatessen with hams, beef roasts, wheels of cheese, cases of beer. People were occasionally shocked by George's habits. He would buy olive oil by the gallon, pour it on his plate and dunk slabs of bread in it; or he would take a quarter-pound stick of butter, peel off the wrapper and eat it like a banana. Perhaps these habits were a residual result of his bitter childhood days when he and his brothers and sister were left close to starvation on the dirt floor of their tiny home. Even so, his voracious approach to food made George unattractive to some people. Babe's friends felt that she had outgrown George, that she preferred the more genteel type of people she met around the golf courses she played. She once bought herself a little Ford convertible that George couldn't fit into, so she could drive to tournaments alone. She tried for years to get him to fix his cauliflower ears, but he refused, saying that they were a badge of his profession and he was proud of them.

Some women on the tour liked George, but others were afraid of him, especially when he was drinking, because he would grab them in playful wrestling holds that often became painful. Despite their often volcanic fights, their discussions of divorce, their frequent separations, Babe and George kept up a constant facade of sugar-sweet love to the public. Yet they fooled no one who was ever around them for more than a few hours; it was strictly a public relations act, and eventually their marriage soured to the point that Babe turned elsewhere for support.

Betty Dodd began playing golf when she was thirteen, but she did not win a professional tournament until after Babe Zaharias died. She was forty-four in 1975, a tall, very slim woman with short red hair, intense brown eyes, the broad shoulders and narrow hips of a young man. Betty grew up an army brat; both her father and her grandfather were generals. Her father, General Francis T. Dodd, was involved in a celebrated incident during the Korean War when he was captured by Communist prisoners at a camp he was running on Koje Island. The incident made headlines all over the world; it embarrassed the American government and General Dodd was demoted to colonel.

Because the family was quite wealthy, Betty did not really need to make a living at golf. Her father, her grandmother and an aunt all left her money after their deaths. She quit the golf tour a few years ago and moved back to San Antonio where she teaches golf. She is an extremely outgoing person, frank, likable and articulate. She speaks in a low voice with a slight Texas twang. Customarily, she wears only two pieces of jewelry, a West Point ring that belonged to her grandfather and the Rolex watch Babe got for her.

Betty first saw Babe when she was sixteen, a junior in high school in San Antonio, when Babe played a Red Cross charity exhibition with Betty Jameson. Students were let out of school at noon to see the match. The next time Betty saw Babe, she was nineteen and Babe was forty. Betty had begun playing on the amateur circuit and she was introduced to Babe at the Miami Country Club. Though Babe was then reaching the peak of her career and was a celebrity of the first order, she immediately became very friendly to the young woman and took her under her wing.

This was not typical of Babe, but Bertha and R. L. Bowen had written to her about Betty Dodd, asking her to help her along. Bertha recalled: "I first saw Betty in nineteen forty-seven. Her shirt was hanging out and her hair was hanging in her eyes, but she was a good golfer. I wrote Babe about her and I guess when they met they liked one another right away. Betty was from a good family and she had many advantages Babe didn't have. But she would go around looking just awful. I remember I came home one day and Babe was giving Betty a permanent. She kept screaming at her, 'Sit still! Bertha made a lady out of me and I'm gonna do the same thing to you!' "

In the fall of 1951, Betty visited Babe and George in Tampa. From then on they were the closest of friends. The two women traveled together whenever they could, stayed together at Lillie's tiny bungalow in Beaumont, at the Bowens' in Fort Worth. Bertha Bowen recalled with a chuckle: "We liked Betty so much, but at times she was so confounded careless about how she looked. She'd dangle a cigarette out of the side of her mouth, stuff her hands in her pockets and slouch around. It was like entertaining a member of the underworld. Betty was lazy, but she wasn't lazy with Babe. When Babe was sick, Betty was a handmaiden to her. And they did have such fun together. They spoke the same golf language and they enjoyed the same things. They were downright professional with the mouth organ and the guitar – 'Begin the Beguine' was a miracle to hear."

There was friction between Betty and George at times. He did not like it that she and Babe were so close. Bertha Bowen recalled: "Betty did not understand Babe at times. She really thought she was going to divorce George. Babe told us that many times, too, but Betty didn't understand that Babe could talk out of one side of her mouth and then do the opposite. I remember when Babe came back from the doctor's office after they took tests for cancer. She was ghastly white. Her lips were just a thin line – as if she had no lips at all. She walked into her bedroom and threw her big brown bag on the chair in the corner and said, 'B. B., I've got it. The worst kind. I'm not worried about myself, but I'm worried about George.' Her thoughts were for him, so I guess she obviously still loved him."

Nevertheless, the support of Betty Dodd was enormously important to Babe—perhaps more than George himself at the end. As her illness became more critical, it was Betty who nursed her, Betty who helped her with the ugly daily medical treatments, Betty who slept on a cot next to Babe's hospital bed during the worst nighttime horrors of the cancer. Many people were convinced that Betty sacrificed one of the most promising careers in women's golf to be with Babe when she was dying. It is probably true, but her loyalty to Babe in those terrible months was worth far more on the scale of human values than all of the trophies and tournaments and money she might have won on the golf course.

Chapter
15

The "People" section of *Time* magazine reported in its usual clipped way in the issue of April 20, 1953:

Golfers in Beaumont, Texas, were not surprised last week when hometown girl Babe Didrikson Zaharias, 39 [she was actually 41] won the Babe Zaharias Open, the local tournament named in her honor. After the tournament Babe entered a hospital for a checkup and doctors ordered her prepared for surgery. Medical diagnosis: A rectal malignancy. Athletic prognosis: the end of a fabulous career in big-time sports.

The end did seem inevitable. One of Babe's doctors, W. E. Tatum, told the Associated Press, "I don't know yet if surgery will cure her, but I will say that she never again will play golf of championship caliber." Never, never again. She was to be condemned to a morbid condition, equivalent to invalidism for someone as intensely active as Babe. After the cancer was found the doctors decided that there was nothing to do but operate. It involved a particularly gruesome surgical procedure with a name that Babe could neither pronounce nor spell at the time: she had to undergo a colostomy. This meant a radical surgical restructuring of her anatomy. The malignancy had to be removed from the rectum, the anus sutured closed, her intestinal tract rerouted so that she passed solid waste through an incision in the left side of her stomach. For a woman whose superb physical condition had been everything for so many years, the psychological devastation of such an operation can only be imagined. Betty Dodd said, "Her mental and emotional state was terribly rocky when the subject of the colostomy came up. She cried a couple of times and kept asking people, 'Do you think they'll *really* have to do it?' Then, after it was done, she accepted it."

Of course the diagnosis of cancer had come as a terrible shock, too. It was a fearsome disease and the actual agonies of it were magnified even more by a general ignorance about it. Although Babe had long been troubled with a hernia, she was rarely ever ill. The early warnings had been clear enough. A couple of months before the diagnosis, she had passed blood. She mentioned this to Betty Dodd, who told her she must see a doctor and added with terrible prescience that this might be a sign of cancer. Babe had put off a physical examination, then finally phoned the eighty-year-old Dr. Tatum in Beaumont and told him of the symptoms. He said that she could wait to see him until she came to town for the Babe Zaharias Open. Babe was delighted at this, but she became more and more fatigued on the tour. Instead of going out to have drinks and dinner after each day's game, she would urge Betty to return to their room and have dinner there in their pajamas. Even after she won the Beaumont tournament, she could not generate any real enthusiasm or energy. Betty recalled: "She was excited but there were no forty-five beers after this victory. My folks had come down to see us play and we went to the room to pick up Babe for dinner. She was still in her golf clothes, lying on the bed. She was white as a sheet and my dad took one look at her and said, 'Babe, we'll send something up for you to eat. You must go to bed.' "

Betty returned to San Antonio with her parents and Babe phoned a couple of days later. "Betty," she said, "I've got cancer. I have to go see a doctor in Fort Worth. Please meet me there." Betty recalled that day: "I got in my car – a brand new one, it was all of ten hours old – and I was halfway to Fort Worth when a gravel truck hit me. The car was a mess and I had it towed to a garage. I called R. L. [Bowen] and he told me that Babe and George had just left because the Fort Worth doctor had told her she had to get back to Beaumont hospital immediately. Well, I'm standing there in the garage, waiting for R. L. to drive over and pick me up when the pay phone rings. It was Babe. She was crying. First she asked if I was all right from my accident and then she said, 'I've got to be operated on. I've got to have a col ... col ...' She couldn't say the word. I said, 'Colostomy?' and she said that's right. It took ten days to build her up for the operation. I moved into the hospital room with her. George was around, but he kept insisting that she *didn't* have cancer."

The operation took more than four hours. The surgeons did some exploratory surgery, too, and when Babe was back in her room, Dr. Robert Moore, the chief surgeon, summoned George and Betty to an office, closed the door and calmly informed them that the surgeons had found more cancer in Babe's lymph nodes. The colostomy had gone well, but he felt that within another year she would have more trouble. He said he thought it might be wise not to mention this bleak news to Babe. Betty recalled, "George was crying. I don't think he heard a word Moore said. I just put the whole thing out of my mind."

Now Babe began her recovery. Betty remained in the hospital room with her. Letters poured in, mail sacks full of them were piled in hallways. Some of the envelopes that arrived were merely addressed "To Babe," not even a city or state on them. Others had nothing but a picture of her pasted on the envelope. Babe's spirits picked up immediately after the operation; she adjusted to the new condition of her body and accepted it. For a week she was fed intravenously and then she began to eat normally again. Betty recalled, "Then she had her first accident. With this type of operation you have no control, you never know when something is going to happen. She had just gotten out of the bathtub and she sat down and everything let go. Instinctively I just put out my hands. It was not that big a thing but from then on she wouldn't let anyone take care of her but me." Babe had to be irrigated every other day and she couldn't do it alone, so Betty helped: they had to keep the opening from healing closed, so Betty would put on rubber gloves and put her fingers in the incision. It was a painful treatment, but it had to be done.

In ten days Babe was up. She wandered around the hospital, visiting the children's ward, talking with elderly people, cheering up everyone she saw. Across the hall was a nun who also needed a colostomy. She refused to have the operation, but eventually Babe was able to convince her that it was not so bad and she agreed. During the course of their stay at Bon Dieu Hospital, Betty suddenly had a hernia attack and she required a minor operation; for a time the two women were recuperating in the same room.

Babe's operation had been on April 17, 1953. On May 18, Babe left the hospital. She and Betty went to the home of Babe's brother Louis, in Newton, Texas. He owned an electrical appliance company there. Babe was recuperating very well, her morale was high and a few days later she wrote to the Bowens: "Dear Bertha and R. L. – Guess what? I am now doing oil paintings and really am surprising myself. Mrs. Nicholson sent me a paint set and I am knocking myself out painting all day and then some. I think when six months are up I will be just as good as new again. I don't feel draggy Bertha as I did before and I am confident that my operation was successful. I am now at my regular weight and afraid if I don't leave Louis and Thelma's soon I will weigh 170 or more." On June 5 she wrote again: "I am feeling wonderful and the col ... y is working okay. I just hope that he will release me so that I can head for home, Tampa that is – you always want to go home, don't you." She stayed in Texas for a time visiting the Bowens, finally returning to Tampa in June. She began to exercise, she began to play golf again. She became stronger every day. On July 31, only fourteen weeks after radical surgery, she entered George May's All American tournament at the Tam O'Shanter Country Club outside Chicago. It was a stunning recovery, even miraculous. Her doctor had flatly declared that "never again" would she play tournament golf ... "never again."

Betty Dodd recalled: "This was so remarkable I still can't believe she did it. We were down in Tampa and Babe said to me, 'Let's go play the Tam.' I told her, 'You're crazy, we haven't hit a golf ball for months.' Well, she was determined. We got up there and she went to the tournament director and said, 'Now, listen, I'm going to play in this thing, but I want to ask you one favor.' He said, 'Babe, we can't let you ride in a cart, you know that.' She said, 'Hell, I don't want a cart, I just want to have Betty Dodd paired with me every day.' This was her first tournament and she was afraid she might have an accident. We had no idea what might happen."

The director paired her with Betty every day. On the first morning of the tournament, they were also with Patty Berg. Babe was nervous, anxious, grim. She had played only eighty-three holes of golf since the operation. She was wan beneath her new tan, a little overweight, flaccid from recuperation. She stuck a yellow tee in her mouth and walked toward the first tee. "Guess I gotta go," she said. Patty Berg murmured "Good luck, Babe." A large gallery had assembled. Babe swung, connected, but did not hit the ball far. The snap was lacking in her swing. She was worried that her artificial intestinal tract might misfunction. Later she said, "You go out there thinking you're going to hit it hard, and then you feel like you're going to pull everything loose and you ease up on it."

She shot an 82 and 85 the first two days of the tournament and got off to a shaky start in the third round. She was under tremendous pressure, but she was unhappy with the mediocrity of her game. Betty recalled the third round: "Neither of us was playing well. She was missing shots and fighting like mad. Then on the fifth hole, she three-putted from four feet. She walked off the green and as we headed for the next hole she sat down on a bench in back of the tee. She just sat down and put her head in her hands and sobbed and sobbed. It was the first and last time I ever saw Babe break down on the golf course. I told her, 'Babe, quit. No one will care. They'll all understand.' She looked up at me with tears streaming down her face and said, 'No, no. I don't want to quit. I'm not a quitter.' She pulled herself together. She hit a fine drive."

George was there, a lumbering anxious bear with his ever-present smoking cigar. He carried a sit-stick for Babe to rest on between shots and he frequently massaged her shoulders. A number of reporters were there covering Babe's comeback, and George kept up a running commentary of insights for them. "If she gets to believe she can do it, she'll be really all right," he said. "It's just like when you sit down to a table covered with food and say, 'I don't want to eat.' Then you eat a little bit and then you eat a little bit more and first thing you know, you're hungry."

Babe finished the tournament in fifteenth place. She scored 82, 85, 78, and 84. In her condition, it was a superhuman performance. The following week she played in the World Golf Championship on the

same course. She shot 74, 77, 75, 81, and finished *third* behind Patty
Berg and Louise Suggs. She won $1,000. In her condition, this was
barely believable. She went on to play the rest of the season. She
finished sixth among money-winners with $6,345.42. She won the Ben
Hogan Comeback of the Year award, nosing out Ted Williams who
had just returned to the Red Sox from marine duty in Korea. She
performed even more amazingly the following year. In 1954 she won
five tournaments, including the U.S. Women's Open at the Salem
Country Club in Peabody, Massachusetts. Her victory at the Open was
the kind of performance that is passed on as legend from generation to
generation: it was a record-breaking triumph in which she shot 72, 71,
73, 75 and trounced her old antagonist Betty Hicks, the runner-up, by
twelve strokes. Babe went on to finish second on the L.P.G.A. money
list with $14,452. She won the Vare Trophy for the lowest scoring
average – 75 over sixty-six rounds. She was voted the Outstanding
Woman Athlete of the Year by the Associated Press, her *sixth* time for
this award.

All this she did with an uncertain reconstructed anatomy – a cancer
victim, publicly condemned "never, never again" to play competitive
golf. In the face of such heroism one might weep or cheer or kneel
down. Of all the things Babe did to deserve her ranking as the greatest
woman athlete of all times, nothing quite approached the grit and
bravery she displayed during her short sensational recovery from her
doctor's fearful prognosis of "never again."

It was not as if she were completely cured or perfectly comfortable.
She wrote the Bowens early in 1954, saying:

I am feeling fine, but still tire easily, but thought I would go and start
the tour anyway. I might get lucky and come through – as I am
striking the ball pretty good – I have to eventually go back to the
hospital and have another job done on the colostomy as I am told that

the tube leading to the opening is too large and I have a hernia in it. When I was in Galveston he had a reservation for me at St. Mary's there but I talked him out of it. He said waiting won't harm me and that if I had it done the same thing could happen in six months. So I just passed. Betty is still wonderful and right with me every minute.

In March 1954 she wrote again:

I'm starting to feel myself on the golf course and think I will be back winning with ease once again. I still get sorta tired on the back nine, but notice it's getting less than before. I just miss the silly easy shots. At this writing I am in second place at St. Petersburg Open. Beverly Hanson has me one stroke, my score, 69, 75 – not bad for a weak old lady.

But 1954 was to be the last good year Babe had. Grim and inevitable things began to happen. In the spring of 1955 she went to Padre Island off the Texas coast in the Gulf of Mexico with Betty Dodd and Betty's sister Peggy. One night they were fishing off a pier until about 11:30 and when they returned to Betty's car, a Lincoln, and tried to drive back to their house, the car sank into the sand, stuck. Betty recalled, "The more I tried to drive it out, the deeper it sank. We borrowed a shovel from two old men who lived near there and Babe started to dig. She was like a demon. The two old men came out to watch and one said, 'God damn, I never did see no woman dig like that.' We'd get the car just about out and it'd roll back down again. Finally we got out. The next morning Babe woke up with a terrible back pain. It got worse and worse. We had to find a nurse on the island for some painkillers. Now that I look back, this was the beginning of the end. The cancer had returned, but it took *months* to find it."

Babe checked into a hospital in Beaumont for tests. Nothing showed up and she left again. The pain got worse and in May she went back to the hospital in Galveston. Betty had gone to the East Coast to play a couple of tournaments, but now Babe pleaded with her to come back to Texas. Betty recalled: "When I got there, Babe was in horrible, horrible agony. They had my cot all set up in her room. When I walked in, she started to cry. They had her in traction but nothing was doing any good. After two weeks, they moved her to John Sealy, another hospital in Galveston. They did another myelogram on her and this one showed a disc problem. The doctors all said, 'Aha, that's it.' They talked about operating. Babe didn't know what a disc operation was going to mean; she didn't know if she was going to have to be in a body cast for months or what. They operated. Nine or ten days after the operation, there was no relief from the pain. She was on drugs and the doctor was about to go on vacation. He finally came in and said, 'Babe, I'm going to lay it on the line. We feel that there is nothing wrong with you. We think you are now addicted to drugs.' "

Babe was stunned, then enraged by this heartless diagnosis. Betty said: "I thought she was going to hit him in the mouth. Here she was in this tremendous pain and he tells her it's in her head, that she's psychologically addicted to drugs. She was just livid. She broke down and cried. Then she refused to take another shot, to prove he was wrong. She was in so much pain she couldn't eat.

"One night when I entered the room I thought she was dead. Intravenous tubes were in her arms, the room was dark. A big German guy was doing nerve blocks on her to try and stop the pain. He left orders for no medication unless he was consulted. She went nuts with the pain. She was in hysterics and started pulling out the tubes. I hit her right across the face and finally got her calmed down. Earlier, a psychiatrist, Grace Jamison, had been called in. She talked to Babe and she told the doctors that Babe was not addicted, that she was not imagining the pain, that there was something very physically wrong. Grace suspected the cancer, but at that point they simply had not found it.

"Finally, Grace saw to it that Babe was put back on painkillers. By now they were x-raying her back every other day. Finally they found it. In the lower spine. A radiologist spotted it, the cancer. In some ways, I wonder if the doctors had kept missing it because they just didn't want to see it. Anyway, it was now just a matter of making her comfortable. There was no way to operate on it."

Babe returned to Tampa with Betty and George at the end of July 1955. Dr. Jamison had given her a metal box with seven different kinds of drugs and painkillers. Nothing more could be done for her. The greatest pain was in her left foot; the cancer had affected the sciatic nerve that ran down her leg and the pain was excruciating. Betty said, "Her foot hurt all the time. The only relief was to squeeze it. I used to lie on the end of her bed for hours and just mash her foot."

Babe's deterioration was by no means swift. During the summer of 1955, she played golf. She would feel very well for a time, then sink into deep pain, which would make her so weak she could scarcely stand. She wrote a letter to the Bowens on October 9, 1955; at the top of the first page was the inked footprint of Babe's poodle, Bebe. The Bowens had just visited her in Tampa and she said:

You know how glad I was to see you both and think you did a great favor to me. I hadn't been up very much until you both came but found out that I could stay up longer than I thought. Now hardly fall into bed at all and am feeling so good. . . . [She wrote about Bebe:] The best thing she likes is riding on the electric scooter. I go out with Betty while she plays and Bebe and I just have a good time, she never jumps off. You never saw Betty hit the ball so good and long. She played yesterday and looked wonderful. I do hope she can really get going next year and make herself good money. I know it takes years to get experience in that old game, and that is all that she needs to be really great. . . . Bertha and R. L. I really don't think it will be too long before I can play again as I am feeling so good and strong. I am having much better nights and the leg is not requiring all the attention that it has needed. *Oh! for the day!* In fact, those long drives of Betty's are killing me. I have to hurry up and play her.

On October 26, 1955, Peggy Kirk Bell visited Babe in Tampa. They played a round of golf, but it was a melancholy affair, Babe's last round of golf. Peggy recalled, "She was in a great deal of pain, but she knew how much I loved to play golf. That gal got out of bed and insisted that we play. She couldn't get her golf shoes on, they hurt too much. So she played in loafers. On the first hole, where she used to drive the green, she shot it about where I did. She did the same thing on the next hole, and she said to me, 'Peggy, you've got to be one of the greatest golfers in the world. How do you break a hundred only driving this far?' She couldn't pound that left foot of hers and it wasn't her old swing. She was in a cart because she just couldn't walk it. On about the fourteenth hole George turned up with some used-car salesman and he told him to go on out there and hit a few with Babe. She always wanted to entertain people, but she just wasn't up to it now. Later she said to me, 'Sometimes George doesn't use good sense.' "

Babe wrote the Bowens about that round:

I am not able to tear into the ball but have to do a lot of figuring so that I can score. Never thought golf took so much thought but it does when you can't hit the tee shot anywhere. I was one under for six holes and bogied the last three both days for thirty-eight, thirty-

nine. . . . Am feeling much better but still suffer the pain in hip and
foot, but think it's getting better by the day. . . . Hope you are able to
read this. I used to take pride in my writing, but now I just scribble.

In early December, Babe returned to the hospital in Galveston. The
pain had increased to a point where she could not stand it. George
scrawled a letter to the Bowens dated December 13:

Mr. and Mrs. Mitchell was here and it mad [*sic*] Babe feel good that he
came all the way from Ft. Worth to see her – and they talked and
talked, all about golf and your swing R. L. Babe is feeling better and
improving every day. And she was hoping & planning to come there
for Xmas. But the Drs. said she may get out after the 1st – So she's all
broken up about it as she was hoping to come there for our
anniversary 23rd & Xmas. She said today Honey I feel better. And she
is going longer without her shots. But takes them for fear of pain. So
Bertha that is all I can tell you. So anything you all decide will be
okay. Any way I'll keep you posted. Give our love to R. L. and
everybody. As Ever Big George.

Babe managed to leave the hospital for Christmas; she and George
visited the Bowens. The day after Christmas, Babe asked to be driven
to a golf course. Laboriously, she walked to the eighteenth green, bent
over and touched the grass with the palm of her hand.

Byron Nelson and his wife brought a cake over for Babe, but she
couldn't eat a bite. Suddenly, she was staggered by agonizing pain in
her abdomen. R. L. Bowen used his own plane to fly her and George
back to Galveston.

From that point on, Babe's life became a deathwatch.

She was in Sealy Hospital in Galveston until the end of January
1956, then to Tampa for a while. In late February, there was a
tournament in Sarasota. Betty was in contention to win it. George

drove Babe over from Tampa in a Nash; he had bought the car because the front seat could be made into a bed. She was thinner, very weak, but she managed to walk to the eighteenth green to watch Betty come in – and lose by a stroke to Betsy Rawls. Betty recalled, "I was dying to win it because Babe was there, but I just didn't. The people on the tour saw her and they knew she was losing weight and that it was hard for her to get around. But nobody came up to me and asked how she really was doing. They were really sorry. I don't think they wanted to know the worst."

Babe's pain came and went in agonizing shock waves. On March 14, 1956, a friend, Triva, wrote a letter to the Bowens:

Babe says tell you she misses you very much. Babe has a pain in her right chest right under her breast this morning and we have called the doctor but he has not gotten to his office as yet. She is having a garden planted by the side of the house and is planting several kinds of vegetables so you will have fresh vegetables when you come down. Please don't wait until the garden grows to come down again. Babe had a real good breakfast this morning and is now up walking around so maybe her chest will be all right. . . .

Nothing was to be all right. Betty was in Tampa with Babe at the end of March. The pain became more constant, more intense; more drugs were required to keep her comfortable. "One day," said Betty, "she was in so much pain she was ready to go back to Galveston. That was it. She never left the hospital."

Sister Lillie moved to Galveston for the final duration of Babe's illness. She took an apartment near the hospital, but she spent many nights either in Babe's room or catching naps in a waiting-room alcove nearby. Her devotion was total. "I fed her and talked to her and at the end she thought it was daylight all the time," said Lillie. "She'd tell me all the time, 'Lillie, you must be hungry, you got to eat,' and she'd get the nurses to bring me coffee and sandwiches and I'd eat 'em and eat 'em till I was stuffed. Oh, I cried so much then. I'd go out of her room and cry and wash my face, and then I'd have to cry some more and I'd wash my face again. Babe, she knew she was gonna die. She held my hand all the time, but she was always thinkin' of others, that girl was. She was all over that hospital when she could still walk. She'd go visit the kids in their wards and fool with 'em and make 'em laugh with her card tricks and things, then she'd say to me, 'Don't go see 'em, Lillie, the kids with cancer are so pitiful. They are there without eyes and without mouths. Oh, it's not so bad for me, Lillie, my cancer don't show, it's on the inside. But the children, some of them, oh, Lillie, they are such pitiful things.' And Babe she would go and give 'em candy and play with 'em for hours and hours."

It took months for Babe's magnificent physique to deteriorate. The letters continued to come in, but in nowhere near the volume they had the first time she had been operated on in 1953. On her forty-fifth birthday, June 26, 1956, Ben Hogan and Sam Snead were playing in the Canada Cup in London and they arranged a moment of silent prayer for her. Players from thirty countries joined the tribute. One afternoon following a L.P.G.A. tournament in Detroit, players and most of the gallery stayed around the eighteenth green after the prize presentation. Betty Dodd began to sing and play her guitar, the crowd gathered around her and she moved to the middle of the green. Someone suggested that people might like to throw some loose change onto the green for the Cancer Fund, in honor of Babe. About $5,000 was collected there that day.

Many reporters were at the hospital to chronicle the progress of Babe's illness toward the end and George arranged frequent press conferences with them. He was usually awash in tears, very theatrical in his presentations. Often he broke down in sobs and had to dash out of the room. The more cynical of the writers reminded each other that although George had not wrestled in years, his talents as The Weeping Greek From Cripple Creek had not been lost or forgotten. Many people felt George turned the hospital into a tasteless circus of grief and bathos.

She sank lower and lower, but so slowly. Bertha Bowen recalled, "They kept Babe alive too long. At the end her teeth were protruding and her face was so thin. She could barely whisper. I guess she never gave up. She kept her golf clubs in the room right to the end. One time toward the end we visited her. R. L. had always kidded Babe unmercifully about how she liked onion sandwiches. This time, as a joke, she wanted to give R. L. this big white onion. She was so weak, she couldn't even hold it in her hand. She had to push it down the bed. We took it home with us. We planted it after she died. We got some seeds, but we were never able to grow another onion from it."

Betty Dodd did not visit Babe during most of the summer of 1956; she was playing the tour, as Babe urged her to do. Betty recalled, "Babe told me, 'Go, honey, and play. Lillie will take care of me.' When I left in June she still looked okay, she didn't start to really lose weight until the last couple of months. But when I came back and saw her in September, eleven days before she died, I was shocked. They had operated for a bowel obstruction and it didn't heal. I wasn't prepared for it, but somehow I managed not to change my expression. She was flat on her back and she had tubes everywhere. She'd had a chordotomy. She asked me to please shave her legs and I remember how thin her legs were – just bone – and I was so worried about cutting her. She recognized me, but not really, I guess. I was like someone way, way back – back in time. I knew it was just a question of days before she died. I was at a tournament in California and Peggy called and said, 'You know, Babe is gone.' I didn't break down; I was past breaking down. I had thought every day for days that I would hear she was dead. When I finally heard, I think I slept for thirty-six hours. I remember going out for lunch in L.A. and all the papers had big headlines saying *Babe Zaharias Dies.* I saw Broderick Crawford stop his car, jump out and then he ran across the street and bought a paper. Then I left for a tournament in Kansas City. I didn't go to her funeral. In the hospital she had said, 'I'd never go to your funeral and I don't want you to go to mine.' Everyone on the tour came up to me and said how sorry they were."

Babe died on September 27, 1956, early in the morning. George held a press conference and he was in paroxysms of grief. Out of this came a series of maudlin sob stories about Babe's death. One such was filed nationwide on the Associated Press wire. It read:

GALVESTON, TEX., SEPT. 28 (AP) – "Babe never really asked God for too much," big George sobbed. He stood in a hospital corridor beside a stainless steel cartload of medicine, cotton pads and steel forceps. Four doors down the corridor, his wife, Babe Didrikson Zaharias, lay dying of cancer which took her life near dawn yesterday.

"When she prayed she asked Him to ease the pain of everyone, not just her own. She never asked Him to win any tournaments for her, she just prayed Him to let her get well and she would do the rest. She never wanted anything but life," Big George Zaharias said, and wept silently as he looked through a window at the blue Gulf of Mexico. By turning her tortured face only slightly the Babe could see the Gulf, too. By now, though even the slight movement of her head was an effort.

"Good God," said George, "I didn't know until right now how great she is! The last round has begun and she knows it's the last round and she's giving it all she's got!" Hours later, Babe opened her eyes and saw big George standing beside her. "I ain't gonna die, honey," she whispered, and gasped. The five words cost a great effort.

They were her final words. Three hours later she slept away into death. It was 6:34 A.M. September 27 and the blue waters of the Gulf outside her window glistened with the sunlight of a new day. . . .

Such lachrymose bunk was beneath Babe's dignity, more fitting to some neurotic Hollywood queen than to a woman who had fought Babe's battles and won Babe's triumphs.

Her funeral was surprisingly small. Fred Corcoran flew down to Beaumont from New York. He recalled, "Not many people were there. Not many reporters. Frankly, there were very few people outside of her family. Patty Berg was there, but she was one of the few women from the tour. I guess women just didn't get on planes and travel back in those days." Babe had wanted to be cremated, her ashes drifted over a golf course. George elected to have a funeral with an open coffin, then have her cremated, then bury the ashes in the ground at Forest Lawn cemetery in Beaumont.

It had taken her a long, long time to die. Her legend perhaps seemed exaggerated in the purple language of obituary and eulogy that followed her death. At times, one might have wondered if it all were really true, if Babe Didrikson Zaharias really was so great. Now more than twenty years later, there can be no doubt. No one has come even close to her in the versatility of her excellence, no one even close to attaining the individual dominance she held over so many sports. Whatta Gal! She was one of a kind; her likes will not be seen again.

Epilogue

The days of Babe Didrikson Zaharias are far behind us, and what has come to pass in the interim? The condition of women in sport has been improved – but perhaps less than one might have hoped. The Ladies Professional Golf Association is rich and successful, though lacking in color and charisma. There are thirty-six tournaments with $2,200,000 in prize money available. In 1975, Sandra Palmer was the leading money-winner with a record $94,805. It is not uncommon for an L.P.G.A. star of the magnitude of Carol Mann, JoAnne Carner, Sandra Haynie, Judy Rankin or Kathy Whitworth to win more than $50,000 a year. Most of the name golfers make at least occasional appearances in television commercials, peddling shirt-collar cleaners and washday detergents to captive masses at home. To make the game more appealing, L.P.G.A. tours are consistently played today on shorter courses, guaranteeing lower scores, which presumably seem more exciting to the public. Had Babe been playing on these truncated layouts, she would be scoring many rounds in the low sixties. Since she died, no one has come remotely close to matching her dominance of women's golf. Amie Amizich, fifty-five, a retired army lieutenant colonel whom many L.P.G.A. members know simply as "The General" has been on tour for ten years as a physical therapist *cum* mother confessor. She played with Babe in the 1950s and said recently, "We don't have anyone on the tour today or even a prospect of another Babe. Oh, how we could use her. If she could just show up, hit one ball and quit, she'd be worth thousands of dollars to us. But, no, there will never be another Babe."

The tennis stars Billie Jean King and Chris Evert possess the nearest thing to Babe's magnitude of fame among women athletes. Televised tennis matches have done much to enhance their reputations – to say nothing of their fortunes. The advent of open professionalism in women's tennis is only very recent: until 1968 "amateurism" was the prevailing condition at all major tournaments and any money forthcoming was concealed in travel expenses and sub rosa payments.

The women's movement – operating with high power and maximum influence for no more than seven years – has caused at least the beginning of a revolution in women's sports. The key element was the passage in the U.S. Congress in 1975 of the celebrated Title IX regulation of the 1972 Education Amendments Act. The major impact of Title IX comes from the legal requirement that any institution (public schools, colleges, universities) receiving federal funds must offer equal programs – and nearly equal financial backing – for both sexes. In short, Title IX promises (though by no means yet delivers) competitive athletic programs for women on an identical level of intensity and excellence as those for men. Of course, Title IX relates only to amateur scholastic sports. Professionally, equality is not even close at hand.

The memory of Babe has dimmed – and nearly disappeared – in the years since her death. In 1975, there was an inexplicable renewal of interest. With no conscious connection at all, in a period of one month our articles were published in *Sports Illustrated, womenSports* (a magazine founded by Billie Jean King) printed a lengthy cover story about Babe by Betty Hicks and CBS aired a two-hour movie about her, which was regettably filled with factual mistakes and fraught with soap-opera clichés.

In 1975 in Beaumont a man named Ben Rogers was trying to collect money to build a Babe Zaharias memorial and museum next to a busy interstate highway. He said he had about $50,000. A high school stadium in Beaumont was about to be named for her, too, but there is no longer a Babe Zaharias Open golf tournament in Beaumont; that had been canceled in 1966 after a shameful episode involving Althea Gibson, a woman who approached Babe's tremendous versatility in sports. Althea had become the first black woman to win the Wimbledon and U.S. tennis championships in 1957. She won both titles again in 1958 and then, in 1963, she switched to professional golf. The Babe Zaharias Open had been sponsored as an annual L.P.G.A. event by the Beaumont Rotary Club for many years. Then Althea entered the Open in 1964. The sponsors accepted her entry – but only on the condition that she could not go into the clubhouse, because she was black. She recalled in 1975, "I accepted those conditions because I was trying to qualify for my L.P.G.A. card. I was not allowed to change in the locker room or even go into the clubhouse for something to eat. I had to change my shoes sitting on the trunk of the car." The following year, the L.P.G.A. tour director, Lenny Wirtz, informed the Beaumont sponsors that Althea was a member of the association and had to be given equal treatment. The Rotary Club pulled out of tournament sponsorship. The Jaycees took over briefly, but they could not meet the financial requirements. The Babe Zaharias Open was canceled after one more year, never to be held again in Beaumont (it is in Cleveland now).

Thus, Babe was fairly effectively forgotten in her own hometown.

Her trophies, once on display in City Hall, were relegated in 1975 to a section at the rear of Finger's Furniture Store, a huge discount market. To see her Olympic medals and her golf trophies, one had to run a gauntlet of salesmen anxious to sell bridge lamps and Naugahyde sofas. In the spring of 1975, a series of sporting events, including a small local golf tournament, was arranged in Beaumont to raise money for the Cancer Fund in Babe's name. During the noon news show one day, a young mod television anchor man interviewed Bob Osius, then the executive sports editor of the Beaumont *Journal* and *Enterprise.* The TV reporter began by saying, "Tell me, why Babe Zaharias?" Osius calmly explained about Babe's career, and as he went on, the television newsman kept saying, "Man, that's *incredible.*" When Osius had completed a thumbnail story of the life and death of Babe, the young TV man exhaled a deep breath and said, "Man, oh, man she must have been some kind of a *legend,* is that right?"

That was right.